My Life Has a Price

To my parents,
Simon and Teni Omaku.
I hope that, up above,
you are proud of me.

My Life Has a Price

Tina Okpara

In collaboration with Cyril Guinet

Translated from the French by Julie Jodter

AMALION PUBLISHING

Published by Amalion Publishing 2012

Amalion Publishing
BP 5637 Dakar-Fann
Dakar CP 00004
Senegal
http://www.amalion.net

First published under the title *Ma vie a un prix* in France by
Éditions Michel Lafon 2010.

Copyright © Michel Lafon Publishing, 2010 *Ma vie a un prix*

Translation copyright © 2012 Julie Jodter & Amalion Publishing

ISBN 978-2-35926-016-8

Printed and bound in the United Kingdom by CPI Group (UK)
Ltd., Croydon, CR0 4YY

Contents

1

A girl in a rubbish bag

Chatou, a commune in the department of Yvelines, France, February 2005.

Rain is falling. My tears are too. The rain falls like a curtain of water, repainting the garden the colour of cement. On my cheeks, the tears are etching streams of salt. My heart is pounding against my chest. I am having a hard time breathing and a hard time thinking. I cross the terrace. One step, one small step. Then another tiny step. Now I am on the lawn. The grass is cold and wet under my bare feet. A gust of wind pastes my green sweatshirt against my body. My long grey skirt sticks to my legs like the skin of an ice-cold rhinoceros. My heart tells me to run, to run as fast as my legs can carry me, with all my might. But I can't. I have the feeling that the tree branches set loose by the winter are going to swoop down on me and push me back with their blackened arms.

I turn back towards the villa. Are they still shouting? Are they still fighting? They are certainly going to end up noticing that I am no longer there. And then they will look everywhere for me. They will take the house apart, search all the rooms. They will slam all the doors, yelling, "Tina! Tina!" They will go down to the cellar, right into my very own hole. They will surely end up looking in the garden and they will catch me. And then…

The booming of my heart rings in my head and all throughout my body. They hit me. They beat me. Tortured me. The fear of dying prevails and pushes me onward. An odour of decomposing plants and earth rises to my nose. This garden smells like a cemetery. I cross the yard without realizing it. An iron fence blocks my way. So I jump. One leap and I land in our neighbour Maria's garden. Without even thinking, I edge through the garden and into the shed where she breeds rabbits.

———————

I stay there, standing, unable to make one more move. I tremble, but not from the cold. The corrugated iron above my head and the straw beneath my feet make me think of an African hut. I can see the verdant valleys, the sun burning so brightly that it bleaches the sky, the roads of beaten earth, the women in multicoloured wrappers and our house in Nigeria. There, I was never cold. There, I was never scared.

I need to catch my breath. I need to control the ideas bouncing around in my head. I cannot stay here, in this shed, amidst the shovels and the rakes, here with the rabbits panicking in their hutches. But I don't know where to go. I would just like to be somewhere else. Anywhere. Far from here. And for everything to stop.

"Is that you, Tina?"

The door opens all of a sudden and Maria is there before me. Sometimes we talk to each other, each one on our side of the fence exchanging bonjour, or saying "How are you?" or "It's nice out today." That's all. For her, I am just a sixteen-year-old girl, her neighbours' daughter. She has never asked me a question. I have never told her anything. She knows that I sometimes slip into her garden to seek refuge in her shed. Up until now, Maria has acted as if she has not noticed anything. Why has she come out to meet me this morning? Why has she decided to speak to me? Because it is very cold and pouring with rain out here? Because she saw that I'm only wearing a skirt and a sweatshirt in the downpour? Or because she heard the yelling a few moments before?

"Why are you crying?" she asks me.

My throat is tight and the words come out of my mouth too quickly. My tears flow thicker. An awful grimace deforms my face and my hands move about in front of me like two panicked birds.

"Help me, for goodness' sake, help me!"

Maria stares at me for a moment. She suddenly seems terrified. She is afraid of them too. I can see it in her eyes.

"I cannot help you, Tina. You cannot stay here."

She doesn't give me time to get one word in. She talks and talks. Impossible to cut in.

"I am a widow! I am a woman on my own!" she yells. "I don't want any trouble!"

And then, continuing to wail, she searches among her tools. She grabs a pair of scissors and a yellow rubbish bag. In the blink of an eye, she cuts a hole for the head and two others for the arms and she slips this makeshift poncho over me before pushing me out of her shed.

"I can't do anything more for you. Leave! Run away now!"

I find myself on the road, in the driving rain. It is almost noon. The neighbourhood is deserted. I walk along aimlessly and find myself in a small park. I sit down on a bench under a tree and keep crying. My head is still spinning…What can I do? Where can I go? Who can help me? I don't know anyone here.

I don't know how long I stay there thinking like this. Ten minutes? An hour? A car goes by on the road, slows down and then stops in front of a house. The door opens and a woman gets out of the car. In the rain, she hurries to open the boot and takes out her shopping bags. Could this woman help me? Or is she going to chase me away like Maria did? I decide to take a chance. I get up and walk towards her. She does not see me coming and startles when I speak to her.

"Madame, at what age does a child have the right to leave her family?"

The woman looks at me a moment and knits her brows.

"It depends," she says.

She looks at me in my rubbish bag dripping with rain, my skirt and sweatshirt soaked by the rain. Her glance halts at my bare feet full of dirt. Then, all of a sudden, she sets down her bags and opens the door to her house.

"Come in!" she says.

Since I hesitate, she insists.

"Come in, I tell you. You are going to catch your death outside in the rain."

The door closes behind me. The woman disappears for a moment and comes back with a white sweater.

"Here, this is for you," she tells me.

I pull on the sweater and follow the woman into her living room. She invites me to sit down on the couch. For a moment, neither one of us says another word. The woman looks at me solemnly and her eyes ask me the questions that she does not yet dare to say.

"Normally, a child can only leave her family at the age of eighteen," she explains in a voice that is calm, so as not to frighten me. "You have to be of age, you see?"

I nod my head. Yes, I understand.

"Except if some serious things are happening in their home," she continues. "If someone is hurting the child…"

Silence. She stares at me as if she wants to read my mind.

"Does someone hurt you at home?" she ends up asking me.

"My father," I answer. "My father hurts me."

The images jostle each other in my head at the moment that I make this confession. The room. The mattress. The pain. The shouts. The blows.

The woman keeps looking at me for a moment without saying anything. Then she turns her back to me and gets the telephone.

"I think that we should call the police," she says.

"No, not the police!" I shout, without meaning to.

"Please," I say more quietly, "not the police."

"Well, what are we going to do?" she asks.

I reach for the telephone.

"Perhaps I could call my house…"

She gives me the phone. I dial our number and tremble while bringing the phone to my ear. One ring. Then another. Then a voice in the earpiece.

"Where are you?"

It's my father. I feel like screaming and throwing the phone against the wall.

"I am outside," I say.

"You have to come home now," he answers.

He is talking in his gentle, calm voice, the voice that he uses when he wants to reassure me.

"Everything is sorted out now. Everything is okay," he continues.

I listen for a moment without saying a word. At the other end of the line, I can hear nothing but his breathing. No hysterical shouts from behind him, no dishes crashing down, no screaming, no threats.

"I'm coming," I say, before hanging up.

The woman followed the conversation standing, watching me, fixed in place like a statue.

"Are you sure that everything is going to be okay?" she asks.

"My father says so…"

She accompanies me to the front of the house and opens the door onto the falling downpour.

"Where do you live?"

I point a finger, indicating the direction in the rain.

"That way…"

"It would be nice if you could give me your telephone number," she says. "Then I could call you from time to time to hear how you're doing. Would you like that?"

"I think it's better if I call you," I answer.

The woman smiles at me. She takes a pencil and a piece of paper and writes down her number.

"You can call me any time. And if anything happens…"

"And the sweater?" I ask.

"You can keep it," she tells me with a sad look.

Her hand touches my arm lightly. I hold on tightly to the piece of paper on which she wrote her number as I leave her house. I head off again, alone, in the rain, a girl in a rubbish bag, a little life only good for throwing out with the rubbish. That is what I have become. My heart starts pounding again and becomes all the more panicked as I get closer to our house. It knows that I am walking towards hell. But I have nowhere else to go.

Oh Mama! Mama! Why did you leave me?

2

The first tragedy of my life

Mama! She goes back and forth in the house. Always busy. Never a moment of rest. She cooks. She cleans. She scolds my brother and me so that we don't get under her feet. She reminds us to finish our homework. My poor mother, Teni Omaku. I close my eyes and I can see her again as if it were yesterday. Holding a wooden pencil between her fingers, she is working hard. Her eyes slide down the paper and she traces a small silhouette dressed in a long skirt, the arms along the body, the hands hiding in the pockets. Mama lifts her pencil. She looks at me, amused. Then she finishes drawing her little lady, adding two points in the middle of the face for the eyes, a small vertical line for the nose and a curved line below. Mama gave her a smile! I watch her wide-eyed with admiration. I am a little girl who is seven years old and, in my eyes, my mother is the best artist in the world.

In the outskirt of Lagos where we live my mother is privileged compared to many: she went to school until primary six. A lot of women from her generation don't go to school. She had also learned the trade of a seamstress, but today she manages a different small business—she prepares food at home that her cousins later go and sell in town.

My father is employed in a factory. Simon Omaku is a modest man who knows how to do everything with his hands. He knows how to drive all kinds of vehicles, even trucks. Papa loves to drive. He is a serious worker. He rents land that he cultivates after the day's work at the factory. He always says that we need the money from the sale of his crops.

We live on the first floor of a building still partially under construction that belongs to my father's boss. There are always lots of people at home. People come and go. There are my mother's cousins that we see going by with huge basins balanced on their heads. My Uncle Bala, my mother's brother, who is always asking if I am doing my homework well. Neighbours who come to talk about football with my father. My mother's friends too. They sit down together to chat about the weather, the prices of things. They complain about men too.

As soon as I have some free time, I run out to play in the courtyard or to play with my friend, Sophie.[1] She is four years younger than I am but we get along perfectly. We spend hours playing and laughing together. Her father, Godwin, is a star, a famous football player. He started out on the team sponsored by my father's boss before being

---

1   The first names of the children have been changed.

taken on in the big clubs in Europe. Her mother, Linda, is a tall, beautiful lady who impresses me a great deal with her outfits and her jewels. You can see that she is rich. Her gaze lingers on Sophie and me when we play together.

"Those two girls, they are like two sisters," she says.

―――――――

Mama's belly is getting round as if she is hiding a big ball under her wrapper. I know that there is a baby inside. If I put my hands on her belly, I can feel it move. What I don't understand is how it got in there.

"How are babies made?" I end up asking.

"Babies come when we sit close to boys," one of my aunts answers, laughing.

I am horrified by the idea that I could also get pregnant. At school, I no longer dare to sit next to anyone but girls…

"Would you rather have a little brother or a little sister?" my mother asks one day.

No need for me to think for long, the answer is obvious.

"A little sister!"

She will be able to share my games. I will introduce her to Sophie and they will be friends. And, above all, I will not be alone in having to help Mama.

Even though I am still a little girl, I have understood for a long time that here men are idle kings. In the house, someone always says: "Tina, do this," "Tina, do that".

But never to my brother, never. Nothing is ever asked of Emmanuel. He neither has to set the table nor clear it. How annoying!

"Why doesn't Emmanuel ever do the dishes?"

Mama shrugs her shoulders.

"It is not boys' work," she answers.

I find that unfair and show it by grumbling, so Mama takes a firmer stand.

"When I am no longer here, you will be the woman of the family! It is a major responsibility, believe me! You must learn now to be responsible and reasonable. When I am no longer here, it will be too late. I will no longer be able to help you…"

Oh, Mama! I have often asked myself why you spoke to me like that. Did you know that you were soon going to leave us? Did you know everything that was going to happen to me? Was it to protect me that you wanted me to be strong, that you asked me to be reasonable and responsible?

When I feel that Mama is too severe with me, I run to take refuge with my father. Papa is always kind to me. I am his little princess and he never scolds me. He gives me hugs and tells me to go and play. I tear down the steps and join my friends in the courtyard.

I pray with all of my strength for the baby to be a girl. A few weeks later, Ayuba is born. A boy! I cry in disappointment. Mother holds me close to her to console me.

"Don't cry," she says. "We will have another baby. And this time, I promise you, it will be a little girl. A little sister just for you."

This Wednesday, the house is full of people. It is the day of the big game on television. The Nigeria national football team, the Super Eagles, is playing against Brazil.[2] All the men are gathered around the television set. My Uncle Bala is there along with neighbours and friends from my father's factory. His boss as well. With the forecasts, bets and squabbles, one can no longer hear oneself think!

"The Brazilians have a better team! They have the great players: Bebeto! Juninho! Ronaldo!"

"The Super Eagles are unbeatable. We're going to win!"

The women shake their heads with a sorry look. Men and their football!

Suddenly, all the faces turn towards the screen. The referee just sounded the kick-off of the game. Just a few seconds later, catastrophe. Brazil score a goal! Arms rise up in the air and clenched fists curse the heavens. My father puts his head in his hands. My uncle strikes his chest. The game could not have started any worse. The game starts again. Lagos, the largest city in the country, the second

---

2   On 31 July 1996, the national football team of Nigeria beat Brazil in the semi-finals of the Olympic Games in Atlanta, USA before going on to win the final against Argentina. The Super Eagles thus became the first African team to win a gold medal in this sport.

biggest metropolis of Africa, holds its breath. The streets are deserted. Suddenly, an immense shout fills the sky.

"Nigeria! Nigeria!"

The Super Eagles score a goal and the game is a tie!

And it continues like that for two hours. The Brazilians score and it's a national tragedy. Then the Nigerians come back and score and there are explosions of joy. On the screen, the players embrace one another and, in our living room, the men leap into each other's arms. Suddenly, even louder shouts make the walls of the house tremble.

"Nigeria! Nigeria!"

The entire country keels over in happiness at the moment when the player Ikpeba scores the winning goal. My father has tears in his eyes. I have never seen him so delighted.

"Why are you so happy?" Mama asks him when, finally, calm returns to the home.

"Because my country's team has won," Papa answers.

A big smile lights up his face.

"And you?" mother insists, "What did you win, Simon Omaku?"

"Women cannot understand," he says with a mysterious look.

———

Mother carries Ayuba on her back, tied to her wrapper. Later, Ayuba takes his first steps. Time passes. Again,

Mama's belly becomes round. Again, I see her stopping and placing her hands on her belly with a grimace of pain. Once more, I pray for a little sister in our family. And then, one morning Mama leaves the house particularly early when I am not yet awake. I go to school, as usual. Upon my return, Mama is still not there. I start doing my homework, all alone. Suddenly, a woman erupts into the house. She is screaming.

"Simon! Simon! Come quickly, your wife is going to die!"

My father rushes up.

"What is happening?" he asks.

"You must come! Quickly!" the woman answers. "Teni has lost the baby! You must take her right away to the hospital!"

A panicky fear invades me. I tugged at my father's sleeve. I want to see my mother. I want to go to the hospital. But my father pushes me back and tells me I have to stay at home. And wait.

"That is no place for a little girl," he explains. "Tomorrow you will go when your mama is better. I promise you."

He kisses me and leaves me there. Emmanuel is allowed to follow him. Why him and not me? I find that so unfair. Even more unfair than the fact that I have to do the dishes and he doesn't!

Mama died that very evening at the hospital.

I hear the adults speaking of fatigue, miscarriage and fate… I don't understand everything and I feel too much grief to ask questions. I am even sadder for not having been able to go and see my mother at the hospital. For not being able to say goodbye to her.

And deep down in my heart, I can't stop myself from asking a horrible question. Did my mother die because she wanted to give me the little sister that she had promised me?

3

Night flight to hell

One day, my father arrives home from work and calls us together.

"Emmanuel! Ayuba! Tina! Come quickly!"

My brothers and I run into the living room where we discover a woman we have never seen before. My father is standing close to her, grinning broadly. He introduces the stranger to us. Her name is Lami. He explains to us that she is going to live with us now, in our house, and that they are soon going to be married. I immediately think that this stranger wants to take my mother's place and my face and heart refuse the situation. I look at the woman. Where did my father find her? How long has he known her? What can he see in her? Wake up, Simon Omaku! Open your eyes! Can't you see that this shrew is just the opposite of Teni whom you cherished so much? Lami is a small plump woman with a sullen look. Mother was tall, thin, lithe, black and perfumed like a branch of liquorice.

Lami is not coming alone to settle under our roof, she brings her three children with her, two girls and a boy that she had with her former husband. Her saleswomen also come to live with us. Indeed, Lami runs a small food business like my mother did. That is their only point in common. Lami manages her team with an iron fist. Every morning, her young employees leave the house with their large basins balanced delicately on their heads. They come back in the evening and give the day's takings to Lami who counts and recounts the nairas, before paying them their salary.

There is never a dispute, Lami wouldn't tolerate that. She is an energetic and authoritarian woman whom it is better not to challenge. Barely settled in our home, she acts like the lady of the house. And watch out if you don't obey her! Even my father watches his step and avoids contradicting her. As far as I remember, I never saw my father and mother fight. With Lami, the quarrels are daily. Over the slightest thing, she shouts, grabs my father by the sleeve of his shirt and shakes him like a palm tree. I do not like my father's new spouse. She understands that well and feels exactly the same way about me. She leaps at the slightest opportunity to yell at me. My father does not dare intervene, even though he clearly sees that Lami favours her own daughters and son at the expense of his children. He surely thinks that, with time, everything will work out all right without any effort.

I often think of my mother. Anything can set off my memory machine: a word, a place, a situation, her writing on a piece of paper or a stub of wooden pencil or the moment when she would have been cooking a meal… all these little nothings take me back and remind me how happy we were before. Then, with my heart heavy, I go and sit down in a corner and let the tears flow down my face. Each time, my father comes running. He puts his arm around my shoulders and pulls me close to him.

"Why are you crying, little Tina?" he asks.

I sniffle and rub my eyes with the back of my hand.

"I miss Mama…"

Then my father holds me tight against him. I feel his warmth, his love. And I forget, a little, that I am so miserable.

Papa always loved Mama, that I know. And I know that he loves her still, even now after her death. I know because, sometimes, when I make myself as small as a mouse and he doesn't think I'm looking, I see him lying down with his face in his hands. And he's crying…

Contrary to what my father thought, time has not eased tensions between my stepmother and me. In fact, conflicts are becoming more and more frequent. I fight with Lami, with her daughters, with her son… I fight with everyone. Our house is now full of shouting and tears. Since my mother died, our home has become a house of misfortune. My father is the first to suffer. I never see him smile as he did before.

I am in the courtyard playing with a friend when my father comes to find me. His face is serious, like when he has thought for a long time and has something important to tell me.

"I have made a decision," he announces. "You are going to go and live with your uncle."

That is not a punishment. On the contrary! My Uncle Bala, who lives on the other side of Lagos, is single and has no children. I love him very much, even if he is stricter than my father. Things move fast. I leave the house of Simon Omaku the following week. A new life begins. Every day I go to school and my uncle checks that my uniform is perfectly clean. When I come home at the end of the afternoon, my uncle is still at work. I am not allowed to go out and play. When he comes home, my uncle checks that my homework is done and my lessons learned. No question of his niece becoming a poor student and I had better watch out if I bring home a bad grade!

Every weekend, my father comes to visit us. I go and wait for him at the bus stop. I tell him everything I have learned at school and he gives me news about Emmanuel and Ayuba. I miss my brothers... our mother's death had brought us closer together. We both avoid talking about Lami. At the end of the afternoon, my uncle and I accompany my father back to the bus station.

"Do you remember Madame Okpara?" he asks me one day as we walk to the bus station.

He lays his hand on my head and strokes my hair.

"She remembers you very well. You will never guess what she proposed."

No. I can't guess. Saying nothing, waiting for what comes next.

"She wants to take you with her in her home," my father continues, "She wants to adopt you!"

"Never!"

I step back a bit. My father is totally surprised by my reaction.

"You will be with your friend, Sophie. And you will have so many nice things!"

I shake my head stubbornly. No, no, no! I am the daughter of Teni Omaku and no one else! I don't want to betray my mother!

My father does not insist but, before getting onto the bus, he gives me a kiss and encourages me to think about it.

———

The next week, he again speaks to me about Madame Okpara and the adoption. My father does not understand my stubbornness. He presents all the advantages that I would have becoming the daughter of this tremendously rich woman. Her husband is a professional football player in Europe, he earns millions and millions. In his opinion, it is a piece of unbelievable luck that they have become attached to me.

"In Nigeria, you will never be able to pursue your studies," my father says to me again. "There is nothing good for you here. If Linda and Godwin take you with them to France, you will have a better life and you can go to university."

After a pause, my father adds these words that crucify me.

"And, in heaven, your mother will be proud of you!"

A few days later, my Uncle Bala asks me to get dressed to go out.

"We're going on a ride," he says.

He makes me climb onto the back of his motorcycle and then goes in the direction of the up-scale residential neighbourhoods of Lagos. Beautiful houses and luxury cars parked along the pavements flash before my eyes.

———————

My uncle stops in front of a lovely double-storey building and makes me get down. Upon our arrival, a guard opens the colossal gate.

"We are here to see Madame Okpara," my uncle says.

I stiffen, but follow my uncle and the guard. My eyes wide open, I can't believe everything I can see around me. This house has all the comforts that we are lacking in our own home and then some… I stand wide-eyed with wonder before the flat screen television that has pride of place in the living room.

Madame Okpara welcomes us. From the way she greets me with a big smile, I see that she is happy to see me again. I ask her for news of Sophie. I would really like to see her, but Madame Okpara explains that her daughter is in Europe with her father, her little brother Steeve and her little sister Sandy. Then she moves away to talk to my uncle, leaving me alone in the living room. I can't hear them, but from time to time Madame Okpara glances in my direction.

Finally, we leave and go back to the house on my uncle's motorcycle.

"You have to get your things ready," he tells me when we arrive.

This time I understand that I have nothing to add. The grown-ups have decided for me. No one asks me for my opinion. My father wants me to go and live with the Okpara family. And my mother wanted me to obey my father.

So one week later, I leave my uncle's house to live in the up-scale area of Lagos. Madame Okpara greets me and explains that she and her husband have undertaken the necessary procedures to adopt me. As soon as the last formalities are settled, I will officially become their daughter and we will leave to join the rest of the family in France.

France, I know where that is… it is far for me. A rich, cold country that makes me dream and scares me at the same time.

While waiting for our grand departure, my existence is completely turned upside down. I have a big room to myself. I eat delicious dishes every day. And what amazes me the most is that here the electricity never cuts out! An incredible luxury. At home, in the poor areas, there were many power outages and you never knew when the power would come back on.

In spite of all of this luxury, I still think of my mother… and I am haunted by the feeling that perhaps I am betraying her.

One morning, I find Madame Okpara in the entry hall, dressed from head to toe and bustling about. She seems stressed and in a hurry. Suitcases wait in front of the house. She announces that she must leave for France to see her husband and settle some business. She gives me a kiss and reassures me. Her brother and a friend will watch over me.

A few weeks pass in this way… The house is strangely empty and quiet. And then, one day, Madame Okpara's brother announces the big news to me. My adoption papers have arrived! He hands me my passport. I open it and discover my new identity. How odd to see the name of Tina Okpara next to my photo.

"You are going to be able to go and join your parents," Madame Okpara's brother tells me. It takes me a few seconds to understand that he is speaking of Godwin and Linda.

My departure is planned for Sunday, 11 February 2001. I only have a few days left to spend here in Nigeria. I suddenly have the impression that I have a thousand things to do. I need to tell my father, say goodbye to my uncle, kiss my brothers goodbye and prepare my suitcase. Oh! But it was quickly ready, my suitcase! A few clothes thrown into the bottom of a small bag, along with two pictures. In one photograph, my father smiles, dressed in a traditional blue *isi agu*[3] and a red hat. In the other, sitting in an armchair, my mother poses in a long ivory dress with a scarf holding her hair back. She also looks happy.

I hold these dear images against my heart and feel the tears coming to my eyes as they do every time I think of my mother. Then I put them away carefully in my bag.

The day of my departure, my whole family, my father, my brothers and my uncle, come to the airport to say goodbye. My father takes my hands in his and he again tells me that I am lucky, that I am going to have a better life and a real future.

---

3   A knee-length shirt worn mainly by people from the eastern part of Nigeria.

"You will pay careful attention Tina," he tells me. "Don't make any trouble. Be a good girl."

What can I say? Huge tears roll down my cheeks. It is so hard to leave your relatives, those you love, not knowing when you'll be able to see them again.

My father holds me tightly in his arms, like after mother scolded me for the dishes or when Lami was nasty to me. He seeks the words to console me.

"Don't cry, Tina," he says softly. "Don't cry… I promise you we'll see each other again soon."

You were mistaken, Papa. You were wrong. We never saw each other again. The last time I saw you was the day that I took the plane to Paris. I was twelve years old. You left to join Mama, your beloved Teni… and I never saw you again, never kissed you again. I was told that before you closed your eyes forever, your last words were for me. You had learned of all the wrong done to me, of everything that I had suffered and endured, and you whispered these words: "I did not see my daughter again…"

———

Night is falling at the airport, making things and people seem all the more unreal and foreign in my eyes… I move away as my father, my brothers and my uncle all wave their hands to say goodbye. My steps are heavy as if my feet are stuck to the African soil. But I move forward, somehow, towards the large iron bird that will take me away from my people. At the entryway to the plane, the stewardess greets me and shows me my seat. Once I am well settled in with the seatbelt fastened around my waist, I can no longer budge. The doors close and soon the plane surges down the runway. I hear the jet engines roaring when we take off from the ground. The city lights become minuscule.

I cry some more, then, exhausted, fall fast asleep as the plane heads deeper into the night. I sleep for almost the whole trip. When I finally wake up, a voice announces our arrival at Roissy-Charles-de-Gaulle airport in French and in English. Here we are!

The plane lands. The cold takes hold of me as soon as I am on the gangway. It is winter here! And I am dressed as I was in Africa, in a simple black, short sleeved T-shirt. I rub my arms to try to warm myself up and I follow the stream of passengers heading towards the exit, holding my precious bag close to me, as if someone were going to steal it.

A small crowd waits in the hall. People find each other, give each other kisses. I look around and suddenly I see who is waiting for me. Godwin Okpara, my new father. He comes up to me and puts the large coat that he brought along for me over my shoulders. Here is the stranger that I will have to get used to calling "Papa". I feel like I will have a hard time in the beginning. He is a bit intimidating. A champion known in all countries, one of the Super Eagles, the national football team that my father, my real father, Simon Omaku, so admired. Tall and strong, you can see that he is an athlete. He also has a very kind, reassuring smile.

"Hello Tina," he says. "Shall we go home?"

I answer with a timid "Yes." How could I have imagined that this man, who smiled at me with benevolence, was going to drive me to hell?

4

A strange family

Never have I been so cold! I'm shivering in the coat that Godwin helped me put on and my teeth are chattering like a frozen old skeleton, making a ridiculous noise of castanets in my head... Try as I might to warm myself up a bit by putting my hands up my sleeves, it doesn't help much. I feel like my fingers have been transformed into icicles. Next to me, Godwin seems to be enjoying himself.

"It is winter here," he announces. "It's freezing!"

He walks quickly and I have to jog to keep up with him in the maze of the airport parking lot. He stops next to a Land Cruiser and opens the passenger door. I climb in and huddle up in the seat while he gets in behind the steering wheel. He finally starts up the car and turns on the heat, which warms me up a bit.

Godwin is not talkative. After asking me how I was, if I had a good trip and if I wasn't too tired, and after hearing the news of the rest of my family, he drives on in silence concentrating on the road.

Fate wanted to inscribe this Monday, 12 February 2001 in my memory so that it would not be forgotten.

We have left the airport for barely ten minutes when a vehicle shoots out on our left. Godwin slams on the brakes and the tyres bite into the asphalt with a strident screech. I feel myself projected forward and my arms stretch out in a reflex, but the seatbelt flings me back against my seat just as quickly. Godwin yanks hard on the steering wheel attempting to avoid a collision. Bang! We crash into something ahead. Godwin swears and parks on the verge. He gets out of the car, then I see him through the windshield speaking to the other driver who has stopped a bit further along. Luckily, there is more fright than damage and we leave a few minutes later.

Outside, the sun is rising. With my nose stuck to the window, I make the most of the light to look at the passing landscapes. Everything amazes me, overawes me. I have never seen such monochrome grey scenery in my life. Grey! Grey! Grey! Everything is sad and grey! The road, the towers, the rows and rows of flat blocks. The trees themselves, bare and thin on the pavements look straight out of an old black-and-white film. Towns with names that look strange to me flash by: La Courneuve, Saint Denis, Gennevilliers, Colombes and, finally, Le Vésinet... Godwin stops the four-by-four, this time he turns off the engine and takes his keys from the dashboard. We have arrived.

"There is your new home," he says to me. "Do you like it?"

Do I like it? To my eyes, it is a real palace. We cross a small garden with a well-kept lawn, then we step into the house. Godwin leads me straight to a large room upstairs. His wife, Linda, is there lying on the bed. She smiles at me.

"Hello, Tina."

I am intimidated and hesitate before entering the room, so Godwin pushes me towards the bed.

"Well, well, you don't want to kiss your mama?"

I move forward and then I see that Linda is not alone in the big bed. She is holding a small sleeping baby next to her, just a few weeks old. I lean over to kiss Linda. I look at the baby. He is sleeping, curled up next to her. She explains that this is the last child of the family, barely a month old.

"What is his name?" I ask.

"Samuel!" Linda answers. "You know, I have always found names that begin with the letter 'S' for my children."

Indeed, before Samuel, there were Sophie, Steeve and Sandy. I'm a bit surprised though. In Lagos, I hadn't noticed that Linda was pregnant. Has it been so long since I last saw her? I try to count the months in my head, but it is hard since I am falling asleep and I fight against collapsing. Godwin realizes this and suggests that I go and rest a bit. We leave while Linda gets up.

My room is a small, well-lit room, with the walls papered in light wallpaper with pink and blue flowers. A real little girl's room.

Outside, it is daylight now. I am so tired that my eyes are closing on their own. I stand by the bed and kneel down, put my forehead on the covers and place my hands together. Eyes closed, my lips barely moving, I recite the Lord's Prayer: "Our Father, who art in heaven, hallowed be thy name…" Then in my head and in my heart, I ask the Lord to bless my father, my brothers and all of my family still in Nigeria and, also, to bless my new papa and my new mama. My head feels heavier and heavier. I get into bed and go straight to sleep.

It takes me a few days to get used to my new existence. The house is so big that sometimes I have the impression that I could get lost in it. There is a garden behind the house and another in front. Each of us has our own room and there are two living rooms, one for the children where we can play and one reserved for Godwin, whom I still have a hard time calling "Papa".

The days seem long, especially when the other children—my sisters and brother—are at school and I am alone. I am anxious to go to school as well, but Linda tells me that it is too late to be enrolled. She tells me it is better to wait till September, in six months. Half a year! I will have to be patient.

In the meantime, I try to make myself useful. I think of my mother, who wanted me to become a "reasonable and responsible" girl. I also remember the advice of my father at the airport: listen well, don't make any trouble. So I do everything they ask me to without making a fuss.

In the morning, I walk Sophie, Steeve and Sandy to their school, an imposing building in white stone with high windows and blue shutters, topped with a slate roof and situated in the middle of a wooded park. Do the children who come here to study know how lucky they are? It is a private international school. All the teachers are bilingual and speak English since, like us, most of the students are from Anglophone countries. Here, like everywhere, maths, languages, history and geography are taught. But the children also discover art, painting and music. The youngest children, like Sandy, have early-learning activities. They are even introduced to cooking through the preparation of little pastries. All of that is expensive of course, but with his salary as a professional footballer, Godwin can easily afford to enrol his three children. And me, when it will be my turn. I look up at the high windows with blue shutters and I imagine behind each one of them children reciting their poetry or working hard on colouring in a drawing. How I would love to be in their place!

When I come back to the house, Linda finds work to keep me busy. It is always "Tina, do this," or "Tina, do that." She asks me to sweep, to mop, to clean the rooms, to do the dishes or to help with the cooking. The tone of her voice is not always kind. I imagine that she is tired from her baby, so I obey, always doing my best to try to relieve her a bit.

Godwin does nothing in the house. He spends a part of the morning with us, but he does not talk much. Then he goes to training and joins the other players of Paris Saint-Germain.

Three weeks after my arrival, Linda leaves us. Indeed, my adoptive mother must return to Nigeria to settle some business. She takes little Samuel along. During her absence, a nanny is hired to take care of the other children. But Linda explains to me clearly that I have to help her and not spend my time in front of the television doing nothing. At the end of the day, when the nanny leaves, I must take care of my brothers and sisters.

One evening, Sophie, Steeve and Sandy are in bed when Godwin comes home with a friend and asks me to prepare the guest room. I obey without asking questions. Then Godwin asks me to set the table and serve some food. Kindly, the young woman offers to help.

"What year are you in school?" she asks to start a conversation.

"I don't go to school," I tell her.

My answer seems to shock her.

"She has just arrived from Nigeria," Godwin says. "Tina is not my real daughter, I have adopted her. As for school, we are in the midst of seeing about her enrolment."

"Do you want me to take care of it?" the young woman asks.

"No, no. I can do it just fine myself, don't worry."

During their meal, I notice the young woman paying close attention to me, when I bring the bread, a bottle of water or anything else that my father asks for.

"Why does this girl have to do everything here?" she ends up asking Godwin. "You can't get up?"

"It is the tradition at home in Africa," he retorts. "You can't understand."

———

That night, I go to bed puzzled. Lying on my bed, I think about what the young woman said. It is as if she planted a seed in me. Why don't I go to school? Why do I have to do all the household work? What are the real reasons for my coming here? For a long time already they have got me into the habit of making everyone's beds and the next morning, when doing the bedrooms, I discover that Godwin's bed was not slept in. Only the bed in the guest room was undone.

A strange family indeed! A mother who travels for several long weeks leaving her children practically alone, a father who makes the most of this time to bring another woman to his home… perhaps it is like this in rich and famous people's houses. I'm going to have to get used to it.

With the summer, major upheavals arrive.

Linda is back just before summer vacation. A few days later, an old lady with a wrinkled face appears at the villa in Le Vésinet. Badejoko Campbell must be about sixty years old. She is an aunt of Linda's, but she considers her more like her grandmother so, naturally, we call her Mamie. She is going to live with us from now on.

Then Godwin changes teams. My adoptive father leaves Paris Saint-Germain for Standard Liège, a Belgian team. And we are going to move. We are going to settle in Chatou, where Godwin and Linda have found their dream home. Chatou. I find the name pretty, even if I don't know where it is. I'm told that it is very nearby, just a few kilometres from Le Vésinet where we live now.

The first days of vacation take place in a feverish, electric atmosphere. Godwin and Linda go to visit their new home. Upon their return, they seem very happy. The children are all excited at the idea of discovering their new rooms, the adults spend their time packing boxes. Linda seems more and more nervous, she screams at me over nothing.

Finally, the big day arrives: a truck takes the furniture and all of our belongings. Godwin takes the children on a first trip. Mamie and I wait in Le Vésinet. Then Godwin comes back to get us.

From the street, we can't see much because a high iron fence, black and grey and as welcoming as a prison gate, almost totally obscures the house from onlookers. Spikes run along the whole stretch of the fence and seem to say: "Nothing to see here! Go on your way!" The left part of the villa, the highest part, ends in a sharp-edged roof with one pitch that slices into the sky. Two windows, as narrow as arrow slits, cut through this modern donjon. An abrupt ramp comes down to the garage, as sombre as the prison cells of a medieval castle. On the right, a flagstone path leads to the other side of the house that is lower and hidden by a curtain of vegetation. Two seated dogs break the horizontal line of the slate roof.

Sophie runs out.

"Tina! Come and see my room!"

She takes me by the hand and pulls me along. We run up the staircase and she leads me to a room full of boxes. A mover is busy setting up my sister's bunk beds. Sophie dances like a crazy little girl and we both laugh. Steeve wants to show me the room that he is going to share with little Samuel so I must follow him too.

In the joyful hubbub, we push open doors discovering cupboards, toilets and bathrooms.

On the ground floor, a large room has a double bed: the parents' room. A bit further along, I discover another room, still empty for the moment. I go in on tiptoes, as if into a sanctuary. It is the only unoccupied room and, quite emotional, I guess that it is my new room.

All day long, we push furniture around and unpack boxes. I help to put away the silverware, dishes and linen.

In the evening, my arms hurt from having carried so many crates and different objects. My legs are heavy from the thousands of steps I must have walked today. I would so like to go to bed but my future room is not ready. It is still empty. Not a piece of furniture. Nothing. I have looked everywhere, but I don't see the slightest trace of my bed.

"Today you are going to sleep on the couch in the living room," Linda declares.

That night, I fall asleep thinking of school. Just a few more weeks of patience and I will finally be able to study. My dreams are filled with blackboards, notebooks and multiplication tables…

The next morning, the room on the ground floor is no longer empty: tons of boxes have been placed in there. Some of them, opened slapdash, spill out Linda's things and clothes everywhere… western dresses, African boubous and wrappers, and tons and tons of shoes. There is no room left, not even for a bed.

I don't dare ask the question. I have a terrible foreboding. Some awful events are being prepared, I can feel it. The night comes. The other children go up to bed. I wait, worried.

"Finish clearing the table and go to bed too," Linda says, then pauses before she adds: "In fact, you can't sleep in the living room every night. You will go and sleep downstairs. For now, that will be your place."

Downstairs. That means the cellar. I barely dare to look at Linda when I answer her.

"Yes, Mama."

I take my things and head towards the door descending to the cellar. Behind this door, there is a staircase with thirteen steps… thirteen steps that I go down slowly, my throat tight, as if I were going underground to never resurface again.

5

Dashed hopes

t is a cold, damp room with tiles on the ground and an electric radiator against the wall. Hung from the ceiling, a bare light bulb sways. Emptied boxes, beaten-up suitcases, a whole range of broken objects are lying about, useless and insignificant. And in the middle of this soulless dumping ground, a mattress has been tossed on the ground with the covers rolled up on top of it. I set my bag containing all of my things on the ground and I get undressed for the night.

I have to go and switch off the light. I'm frightened. Scared to go to the door, turn off the light and come back. And yet, I have to. With one finger on the switch, I estimate the distance that separates me from my bed. Four steps? Five? I take a deep breath. Click! Here I am, plunged into darkness. Clumsily, I approach the mattress with hesitant steps. I sit, but I don't dare lie down yet.

There is no noise around me, or rather, no human noise. Just the rumbling of the pipes and some metallic gurgles. All the reassuring signs of life, all the warmth of the others has disappeared entirely. A feeling of immense and desperate isolation takes hold of me. That night, I do not kneel at the foot of my bed. I do not place my head on my united hands, my eyes closed. For the first time in my life, I do not recite "Our Father". I lie down, trembling with fear. I think about my father… my real father. I think about my mother. I think about my whole family, back in Nigeria. Why did they abandon me? Why did they give me to this family? Did they know what would happen to me? My father! My uncle! Did they lie to me to make me fall into a trap?

The first night in the cellar, I pull the quilt right up to my nose to stop inhaling the musty smell and I fall asleep with my face bathed in tears.

The next day, Linda tells me how to spend my day.

"Get the broom and follow me!"

We go upstairs and she explains what she expects of me. I have to tidy the rooms and vacuum starting with the room in the back. Once the rooms are done, I must sweep the staircase and then, having arrived below, do her room, continuing into the living room and finishing with the kitchen. I set myself to work without breakfast, but I dare not ask for it. Hunger gnaws away at my belly.

All day long, Linda tells me, as time goes by, what I must do. After sweeping, I have to do the dishes, then the ironing, the shopping and the cooking… and she categorically forbids me from using the washing machine for the laundry.

"You are too stupid," she tells me. "You would be capable of ruining the washing!"

I spend the two months of the summer holidays working in this way, all day, from morning to night. I eat when I can… alone in the kitchen. I have the feeling I am going to go crazy. I hang onto one last hope… each day that goes by brings me closer to the moment when I will go back to school.

But then Linda does her shopping for the start of the new school year and passes out notebooks, pencil bags and pencils… and there is nothing for me.

"I'm not going to go to school?" I ask.

Linda strikes me down with one look.

"You? You want to go to school?"

"I have to go to school," I say, surprising myself at holding my head up to her.

She bursts out in crude laughter.

"What would you do at school? You're stupid! You think they take dunces at school?"

I am petrified by her words. My lips tremble.

"You are just good for sweeping and even for that, we always have to be behind you!"

She comes up to me and assumes a disgusted look. All the disdain that I inspire in her is visible on her face, in the flared nostrils of her nose, on her wrenched-up mouth.

"And you stink! It's just not possible to smell so bad! How do you expect them to accept a girl who stinks this much at school?"

She steps in my direction and, instinctively, I cross my arms over my head in a defensive reflex.

"From now on, you will get up earlier in the morning to take a shower! I don't want to smell this repugnant odour any more."

I am no idiot. I'm not as dumb as Linda thinks. And I know that this story of odour is only a pretext…

Do you want to know what my days are like? Really? I have to get up early. Because, since she declared that I stink, Linda gave me an alarm clock that I have to set for five o'clock in the morning. I get up when the whole house is sleeping and I take my shower.

Next, I iron the children's uniforms and get their shoes ready. They must be spotless. I verify that nothing is missing in their school bags. Then I go to the kitchen and prepare their breakfast: a bowl of chocolate milk, toast, butter and jam or cereal. I go upstairs to wake up Sophie, Steeve and Sandy, then help them take showers and get ready. I rub body cream into their skin and get them dressed. While they eat their breakfast, I prepare their snacks of fruit juice and biscuits that I will put into their school bags later.

Hurry up! Now it's time to leave for school. The Okpara children still go to the international school of Le Vésinet.

From Chatou it is a forty-five minute walk to reach the big beautiful white stone building with blue shutters. I drop off the children there and come back running with Sandy's stroller in front of me, empty and rattling. Better not to dawdle if I want to avoid Linda's scoldings.

Once back, I start the housework. I make the children's beds. Linda demands that I change the sheets twice a week. I do the laundry, then I hang it up to dry.

Are you still following me? Soon it will be noon. Luckily, the children eat at the cafeteria so I don't have to go and get them. I then attack the sweeping of the steps. As a rule, just at that moment, a roar reverberates throughout the house.

"Tina!"

This shout means that Her Majesty Linda has just woken up. She's hungry! She lazes about in bed a bit longer, then gets up, in a bathrobe or a wrapper and goes to lie in front of the television.

"Tina! Are you coming today or tomorrow?"

I arrive with a tray upon which I've placed her cutlery and her favourite dish, a plate of spaghetti covered with a sauce cooked with peppers, onions and seafood. But she can also decide otherwise. I see right away from her mood when I arrive with the tray if she is going to send me back to the kitchen or not. If her grimace is sullen and her stare threatening, she is going to yell:

"What is this rubbish? You think I'm going to eat this?"

Then I have to turn around! I make something else, sometimes with Mamie's help. Linda waits in the living room, sprawled on the couch. When she gets up later she will go to find dust on a shelf or scold me for not having finished one task or another… She'll shout at me, perhaps hit me, before leaving to go shopping or for a walk with a friend.

At the end of the afternoon, I leave to pick up the kids at school, then I make sure that they do their homework. After supper, I put them in pyjamas for the night and put them to bed. My day is not yet finished. I still have to serve Linda and Godwin and their guests if they are having people over. Godwin has perhaps invited another player from Paris Saint-Germain, Linda may come home with a friend. Whatever the time, be it midnight or even later, I have to be there.

And my lunch break in all that? You will have noticed that I didn't mention it in my schedule? Because I don't have one! I eat when I can, when Linda is out, or when the hunger torments me too much. I eat standing up in front of the stove or sitting in a corner. Never a hot dish. I am only allowed to have leftovers.

A few weeks of this life have transformed me incredibly. I've made myself a shell to block slaps, deprivation, anger, humiliation and insults. I've become used to not talking since they practically do not speak to me all day…

except for barking orders. "Do this! Do that!" And all that I get to say is: "Okay, Mama."

The only thing that my body cannot get used to is the fatigue. The lack of sleep is literally crushing me. I sometimes have a really hard time keeping my eyes open.

My state seems to worry Godwin.

"Why are you always like that?" he asks me one day.

"Like what, Papa?"

"Well, you drag your feet and walk along like a zombie as if you are always sad and tired!"

What can I say? Doesn't he see what is happening under his own roof? How I am treated from morning to night? Doesn't he know who wakes up the children, washes them, dresses them and takes them to school? Doesn't he know who takes care of his house, keeps the linen clean and changes the sheets? Has he ever asked himself who mows the lawn?

He knows perfectly well! The other day, he came home with the boot of his four-by-four full of logs. He asked me to unload it and he stood next to me, without making the slightest move to ease my pain, without carrying a single log. A neighbour witnessed the scene from the other side of the fence. I saw that she was watching us, me working hard, Godwin with his arms crossed, and that she seemed shocked.

"I am sad because I would like to go to school," I tell him.

"This story again!"

"I was promised…"

"I'm going to speak to Linda."

He smiles at me.

"I promise you that I am going to try to talk to her about it," he says again.

I know that he will never manage to convince her. Godwin Okpara is perhaps a great footballer, an international defender. He is perhaps cleverer than the opposing attackers, no centre-forward scares him, but he can't stand up to his wife! She is seven years older than him and one head taller. She dominates him physically and psychologically.

I don't blame him. Godwin, at least, has a good side. When he is there, Linda doesn't hit me. Indeed, the blows have come to be added to the insults for some time. If she raises her hand against me, he intervenes right away.

"Leave her alone."

Linda insults me, spitting her venom.

"Why do you protect her? Are you sleeping with her?"

Godwin shrugs. I slip away quietly. In those instances, she does not open my scalp by hitting me with her high heels. At any rate, she knows that she will get her revenge later.

All occasions are good for humiliating me, putting me down. All day long, she repeats how stupid I am, an idiot, that I smell bad, that I am just an animal.

One night, I am in the middle of ironing when I hear Linda come in. She complains to Mamie that there are too many people in the shops. She is exhausted after having walked around all afternoon. She seems in a bad mood. A little while later, as I expected, she shouts my name. I leave my work on the ironing board to hurry to the living room. Lying down on the couch, Linda turns on the television with the remote control and hurls a scornful look at me.

"Go and get my massage oil," she mutters.

When I come back with the bottle in my hand, she hitches up her dress, revealing her legs to the knees.

"Massage me!" she orders.

I kneel down and obey. I don't know how to go about it and her big feet, her huge calves disgust me. I'm loath to touch her. I start by pressing her toes between my fingers, I continue with the soles of her feet. She says nothing, captivated by the film that is starting. Little by little, I see her eyelids get heavy, her eyes close. I massage her a few more minutes then, noiselessly, I get up.

"Who told you to stop?" she yells, suddenly opening her eyes.

I throw myself down on my knees and start massaging her again. She demands that I also massage her calves and her thighs. These enormous chunks of meat disgust me, but I obey. I don't have a choice. I continue all throughout the film. The credits have just barely begun to scroll across the screen when she gets up and leaves the room without a word.

There are never thanks for Tina in this house. There is never anything for Tina! When Linda comes back from shopping, she calls me so I can put things away. She empties the bags, separating the different purchases by saying, "That's for the children, that's for Sophie, this is for me." I then know where I have to put things away. Never does Linda say: "This is for you, Tina." This sentence doesn't exist. There is nothing for me. I have nothing of my own. My wardrobe consists of used clothes. The furniture in my room is limited to an old box in which I place my things. What little I own is made up of things that have been thrown out and I have managed to retrieve. It was in such a way that one day I find a notebook in a rubbish bin. The cover is worn and a few pages are missing... but it is a treasure to me. With my heart beating strongly, I hide it under my T-shirt and hurry to bury it in the depths of my box, under my clothes. I think of this notebook all day long. I can't wait to go and find it. It is like a friend waiting for me. That evening, as soon as I go downstairs, I hurry and start to write—pinching a pen was not very complicated. My first words are for Linda. "She hates me. She treats me like an animal." I have a hard time tying my sentences together. Everything jostles in my head and at the end of my pen. I would like to write down all of my rage, my hate, my solitude.

"She remains for hours in the toilet. I can hear her on the telephone with her friends. Is she ashamed? No! She is ashamed of nothing. She doesn't even flush the toilet when she's done! And I'm the one that has to do it when I clean the room!"

Writing does me so much good that, in spite of my fatigue, I always find the energy in the evening to confide in my notebook. I write a few lines or a whole page. I tell the events of the day. I take it out on Linda. Then I put away my precious notebook, my only friend, under my clothes, in the box, convinced that no one will come and look for it here.

6

The secret notebook

I have never heard Linda Okpara say "I love you." Not even to her children. When she wants to show them some affection, she gives them a gift, buys them a toy or takes them to eat at McDonald's. The rest of the time, she doesn't want them around her.

"Go and read in your room!"

How many times have I heard her pronounce those words? The children should not disturb anyone and definitely not make any noise. It sometimes happens that she will be interested in their homework. Then she picks up a notebook, looks it over, asks one or two questions and it always finishes in the same way. She yells! Because they have given a wrong answer, they have a poor grade, or they haven't learned their lesson. She never sits down next to them to do a problem again, she never takes the time to explain a poorly understood lesson to them. They have to know and understand everything right away! This woman is full of impatience and fury. There is no room in her for tenderness and maternal love.

We are five children in the Chemin des Petits-Chênes villa. The house should be full of laughter, cries of joy and the sounds of squabbling. There is none of that. There are only Linda's rages and screaming.

The children have understood that I am not treated in the same way as they are. I think they suffer from it. One day when his mother hits me, little Sandy gets squarely in the way. Poor little one! She hurries into my arms crying my name and begging her mother to stop. That doesn't prevent Linda from continuing to thrash me. I therefore have to protect Sandy who, huddled in my arms, is at risk of receiving the slaps destined for me.

Sophie also pities me. To see me slaving away all day long makes her heart hurt and she tries as soon as she has time to relieve my burden. She manages to dress herself alone while Linda insists that I help her. In secret, she sometimes helps me fold the laundry or wipe the dishes. Watch out if Linda surprises her with a dish towel in her hands!

"Sophie! Get out of there. That is no work for you!"

And in passing, that day, I get a slap. With my cheek stinging, I come down to my "room". Sophie follows, feeling sorry for me though it is not her fault at all. She should not feel guilty and I tell her that. We stay there a minute talking as we do sometimes. I am her confidante. She tells me stories about her days at school, her problems with her friends. She also talks to me about boys, the ones she finds cute. I listen to her. I envy her having a life outside of this house.

That day, while we are chatting, I am not paying attention when Sophie looks into my box. Suddenly, I see her knit her brows, then reach into my things. Before I can make the slightest move, she grabs my notebook, opens it and starts to read.

"What is this?" she asks.

It takes me a few seconds to react. I hurry to Sophie and grab my diary from her hands, but it is too late. She has had the time to read a few passages.

"You dared write that about Mama?" she asks, incredulous.

She looks at me, half amused, half admiring, at least so it seemed to me.

"Don't worry," she tells me, "I won't say anything. To anyone!"

That evening, for once, I have good news to write down in my notebook. Magda and Patrick are coming to spend a few days at the house! I take my pencil and write: "These are the best people I know. When they are here my life is less tiresome."

Magda and Patrick are from Brussels. They met the Okpara family in the early 1990s when Godwin went to play in Belgium. At that time, he was even awarded the Belgian Soulier d'ébène, given to the best player of African origin. Years later, Godwin was transferred to France, but Magda and Patrick kept their ties to my adoptive father. They call each other regularly to hear how we are doing and sometimes, to my great joy, they come to spend a week with us bringing their children who are close to my age.

Magda has short brown hair, the face of a courageous woman, a smile full of kindness and eyes that overflow with tenderness. When Magda is here, my lot improves. Linda doesn't dare treat me badly in front of her. She makes me do less work, harasses me less often. No slaps. No insults. No shoe blows to the head. Throughout her stay, Magda takes care of the cooking—that much less work for me— and the house is full of pleasant smells. Of course, Linda makes sure that I don't sit at the table at the same time as everyone else, but Magda always leaves me a plate inside the microwave oven. I only have to heat it up to enjoy a good meal. From time to time, she leaves me some change or places a coin or a note in my hand with one finger on her mouth. Shhh!

Even more than my stomach, Magda warms my heart. When she speaks to me, when she addresses me, I feel love, respect. She treats me as a human being. I think that she is not taken in by the charade. She understands that I am not treated as an equal to the other children of the Okpara family.

"Are you unhappy at your parents' home?" she asks me one day when we are alone in the kitchen.

I lower my eyes. Magda comes close to me and bends down. Her face is close to mine.

I slowly nod my head.

"I would like to go far away from here," I say.

"Listen," she tells me, "I don't know the law in France. I don't know at what age a child can leave his family."

I shrug my shoulders. I don't know what to say. Where could I go if I left this nightmare of a house? I don't know anyone. I speak French very badly. The few times I have tried to talk with a neighbour, I see that they have a hard time understanding me. I am trapped.

My throat tightens. It hurts in my chest, as if someone was squeezing my heart in their clenched fist. It makes me even sadder to see Magda's eyes become blurred and a tear slide down her cheek. She's crying. Because of me, she's crying. She gets a tissue out of her pocket and wipes her eyes.

"I'm going to find out," she says. "Linda and Godwin adopted you. It's complicated. You can't be taken away from them so easily."

The next day, at the moment they leave for Brussels, Magda kisses me and holds me close.

"Be strong! Be courageous!" she whispers to me.

Again, it seems that her glance waivers. She kisses me one last time on the forehead and speaks softly in my ear:

"I will always be there for you…"

With Magda and Patrick gone, I return to my daily hell.

———————

I can't remember why anymore, but that day I get into a fight with Sophie. A trifle. A childish quarrel of no importance. It does not seem significant to me at the moment.

"I'm going to tell Mama!" Sophie screams angrily.

She turns on her heels and runs off, furious. I shrug. I think I reply that I don't care. I don't remember the details. I pick up the vacuum again and get back to my work. A few minutes later a scream shakes the walls of the house.

"Tina!"

I hurry to the living room. Linda is there waiting for me. Her eyes are shooting lightning bolts of hatred, worse than ever before. Behind her, Mamie gives me an unpleasant stare. I tremble like an animal caught in a trap.

"Is it true that you have a notebook?" Linda asks me.

I want the earth to open up, right there, beneath my feet. I would like the ground to swallow me up. To disappear. To faint. To vanish. I don't answer. I start crying, in silence.

"Is it true that you have a notebook?" Linda repeats, her eyes leaping out of her head.

"Yes…"

"Go and get it! Right now!"

I feel like all my strength has left me. I go down the stairs. Sophie told on me! For a simple argument! For a childish jealousy! Sophie told on me and now I am going to die… I am certain. It is the last time that I will see this squalid cellar that is my room, that I will breathe this smell of mould.

I take my notebook and walk up the stairs as if I am going up to the gallows.

Linda, to me, is like a queen, which is to say that her will dictates my deeds, my every move. She is all-powerful. What she wants me to be, I am. And when she reads what I have written in this notebook, she will want me to be dead.

Upon returning to the living room, I hand her my diary. She rips it out of my hands and leafs through it right away. She lets out demented screams while turning the pages.

"You know what she has written?" she yells at Mamie, holding the diary above her head.

"You know what could happen if someone came across this one day?"

She throws the notebook to the other side of the room.

"You piece of rubbish, you want to send me to prison!"

Mamie goes to pick up the notebook. I am crying so hard that I see the whole scene out of focus through my tears. A pain rips at my head. Linda has just hit me with her favourite weapon, a shoe. A white Dior pump. The high heel has torn my scalp. She hits me again and yells.

When she tells me to disappear, I hurry down to the cellar and throw myself on my mattress.

I run my hand through my hair. The sight of my own blood horrifies me. I'm scared. I'm hurt. I'm bleeding. And yet, I must not scream. I must not make any noise. She must not hear me.

The next day, when my alarm goes off at five in the morning, I get up and hurry to take a shower. Then I go upstairs and search through the rubbish bins, expecting to find the remains of my notebook. What hurts the most is that between the pages of the notebook, I have left the photos of my mother and father. In my panic the day before, I didn't think to take them out and hide them away from Linda's fury. I have looked all over and I can't find any trace of the notebook or the photos. So much the better! That means that they are hidden somewhere, but not destroyed.

All day long, when putting things away for everyone, I make the most of the opportunity and look around for my belongings. In Mamie's wardrobe I find my photos. They are there, hidden in a pile of linen. On the other hand, there is no trace of my notebook. It has purely and simply vanished.

A few weeks later, I again find a small spiral notebook abandoned in a rubbish bin. Only half of the pages have been used. I hesitate just a moment, thinking of Linda's fury. But I miss writing so much! I need to pour out my overload of troubles, my desperation, onto paper. So I take the notebook, I rip out the used pages and again I slip it under my T-shirt. This time, I will make sure I hide it well. And in the evening, before going to bed, I return to my habit of writing about my misfortunes.

On the other hand, I no longer pray. It is not me who has forgotten God, but He who has forgotten me.

7

A broken childhood

February 2003. I have now been the slave of the Okpara family for two years. Two years that I have worked for them from morning to night and slept in their cellar. Two years that I have prepared their meals and eaten only leftovers. Two years that I have taken care of their children, that I have kept their house clean, that I have washed, ironed and put away their laundry. Two years that I have massaged Linda's fat legs and flushed the toilet when she has finished relieving herself…

Two long years of captivity, exploitation and humiliation. I am fifteen years old and I am no longer a human being. Just a shadow of myself remains. Everything about me has been extinguished: my eyes, my voice, my smile. Physically, I have become a zombie with fleeing eyes, crushed by fatigue, floating about, ridiculous and pitiful, in clothes that Linda gives me that are often too big, worn, old and out of fashion. Psychologically, fear and desperation have broken me. Resigned to it, I survive only by stealing my food and managing to sleep a few moments when I can.

My isolation is total. I have never been to school since my arrival in France. I have no friends, no one to confide in or speak to. How could I anyway? I am not allowed to go out and I don't speak French!

During the rare outings in which I participate, I remain under Linda's constant surveillance or the insidious spying of Mamie. Since two missionaries came to canvass at the house, we regularly go to the Church of Jesus Christ of Latter-day Saints[4] in Versailles. If I go with Mamie, it is above all to take care of the children. Linda or Godwin drives us there and comes back to pick us up after the service.

At least the outing allows me to leave the house a bit, to escape my daily hell, to hear about God and to see some new faces. At the exit from the church, Mamie sometimes speaks to other people and lets her vigilance slip. One day when she is busy talking, I make the most of the moment to move away and go up to a group of adolescents my age. To my great surprise, they are speaking English. They are curious and want to meet me. The questions come from all directions. They want to know what my name is, where I come from, what school I go to…

---

4   The Church of Jesus Christ of Latter-day Saints is a Christian church founded by Joseph Smith in 1830. The Mormon church numbers an estimated 13 million faithfuls from all over the world.

I don't have time to answer. Mamie, sensing danger, comes up. She replies on my behalf. I don't go to school, I follow classes from home, I work on the computer. Then she hurries me away from the other young girls. Finally, certain that no one can hear us, she gives me a lecture. I must not speak to anyone. Say nothing! Never! Or else…

And yet people from the Mormon church discovered in what conditions I was living and without my needing to tell them. One day, Mamie invites a church friend and her daughter Sonia, a teenager who is my age, to have tea at the house. Without me noticing, Sonia follows me right into the cellar.

"It's horrible here!" She exclaims upon discovering the mess in the cellar. "It stinks of mould! It smells rotten!"

Then she notices my "bed". By this time, I had saved a door that Godwin and Linda had broken when fighting and put it under the mattress to try to insulate myself from the dampness of the ground.

"You sleep here?" Sonia asks with astonishment.

"Yes, it's my room. This is where they let me sleep," I say. "When I am eighteen, I will leave and they will never see me again!"

"You are so right!" Sonia says to me, "I'm with you all the way!"

Did Mamie notice that Sonia visited me in the cellar? Without a doubt. Sonia and her mother were never again invited to the house.

Linda can come into the house at any time, in the middle of the afternoon or late at night, alone or with someone. Whatever the hour, however many guests she has, I have to be available and set my work aside immediately to be at her service. Most of the time, she asks for something to eat.

That is the case today. At the end of the morning, my adoptive mother enters the house like a tornado. A man I have never seen before is with her. Linda introduces him to Mamie as a childhood friend and asks the children to call him "Uncle". He is not very talkative. You could even say he wants to avoid us.

Linda orders me to prepare something to eat for them and disappears into her room. When she comes back out, she has traded her boubou for a provocative outfit. When she walks her dress opens up to the top of her thighs. It is so indecent that I dare not look at her any more. After lunch, Linda takes her guest into the guest room. They stay closed up in there together for some time. When they reappear, at the end of the afternoon, Linda announces that they've decided to go out for a bit and they leave as suddenly as they arrived.

Night has fallen and Linda and Uncle have not yet come back. I've showered the children and am getting ready to feed them supper when the telephone rings. I pick up the phone and recognize the voice of Godwin on the other end of the line.

"Tina! Pass me Mama, please."

"She's not here," I answer.

"Where is she?"

Something tells me that I had better be cautious.

"I don't know," I say.

"Pass me Sophie!"

I call Sophie and give her the phone.

"Papa wants to talk to you."

I stay next to her, dreading something. I hear Godwin's voice crackling in the earpiece. Sophie answers "yes" then "no" two or three times... I can't wait for her to hang up. I would like her to understand that she shouldn't talk about Uncle. But then, suddenly, she says these fateful words:

"Mother went out for a walk with Uncle."

I try to make a sign for her to be quiet, not to say anything more, but it's too late. On the other end of the line, Godwin interrogates Sophie. She answers him innocently. No, she doesn't know Uncle. No, she had never seen him before, it's the first time that he came to the house. Yes, he's nice.

Sophie hangs up. I remain there a moment staring at the phone as if a catastrophe was going to come out of it. Luckily, Godwin is in Belgium, far from here. God only knows what would have happened if he were here in Paris! Linda comes home just a few minutes after this telephone call. Uncle is still with her. She seems very happy.

Even when Sophie tells her about her father's phone call, it doesn't eat into her good mood.

Next, everything happens very quickly. Suddenly, the front door swings open. In the frame of the door, an athletic body that I know well appears. Godwin! What is he doing here? Why isn't he in Belgium?

I understand everything in a fraction of a second. He was on his way when he called, it was a trap!

I am expecting lightning to strike the house, a hurricane of screams and shouts. And yet, nothing like that occurs. Linda, slightly ill at ease, introduces her "childhood friend" to Godwin. Uncle holds out a hesitant hand that Godwin shakes, his jaw tight and eyes bloodshot. The evening passes in a heavy and tense atmosphere. Uncle spends the night in the guest room and disappears the next morning.

After his departure, Godwin orders me to take the children to the small living room upstairs.

"No one can come down until I say so," he growls.

I group together Sophie, Steeve, Sandy and Samuel upstairs and make sure that they don't try to go down. But they have no intention of doing so. The explosions of rage coming up from the ground floor are much too frightening. Screams. Insults. Crashes. Godwin and Linda scream enough to make the walls shake and I hear everything they say. I can thus recreate what happened.

Godwin went over the bank accounts with a fine-tooth comb and discovered that his wife was making unusual expenditures. Why? For whom? Godwin conducted his own inquiry and discovered that Linda was having an affair with another man. She even gave him a large sum of money so that he could rent a flat. Mad with jealousy, Godwin had the idea of coming home unexpectedly to catch her red-handed. On her side, Linda denies it. She screams. She asks him what he does at night when he is alone in Belgium.

"Poor bastard!" she yells. "Our marriage is over!"

The front door slams and we hear a car start angrily a few moments later. Linda is gone. Only silence remains, a heavy oppressive silence. The house itself seems to be holding its breath.

I go down to the kitchen to start putting some order in the battlefield. I pick up chairs that were sent flying. I pick up the remains of a cell phone that exploded against a wall. Godwin must have taken refuge in his room behind a closed door.

Mamie soon joins me. With a serious and sober air she examines the area like a police inspector looking for clues.

"Mama will not come back tonight," she announces.

"You can sleep on the couch in the little living room if you like," she says.

I make the most of the opportunity, too happy to abandon my cold and dank cellar for once, but not really reassured. At any moment, I expect to see Linda reappear, furious. If she finds me there, she will take it out on me. No doubt about that.

I ask myself if I am going to manage to go to sleep, but, contrary to my fears, I fall asleep moments after lying down. Until I hear a noise. Is Linda home? No! In the shadow, I see Godwin's silhouette. He is watching me.

"Get up and come with me," he says.

What time could it be? How long did I sleep? What is happening? I am so tired that I have a hard time organizing my thoughts. I get up and follow him like a sleepwalker. He heads towards the door that leads to the cellar. I go down the steps after him. Arriving downstairs, he turns on the light. The sudden brightness makes my eyes blink.

"Do you know what is happening here?" Godwin asks me.

Since I refuse to answer, he insists.

"Do you know the man who was with Mama?"

"No."

"You know that he is her lover?"

"No, I didn't know."

I would like to go back to bed. Why did he make me come down to the cellar to talk about this with me? I am just a girl. Why don't they manage their problems between adults?

"Have you already thought of your future later? What you would like to do?" he asks me again.

I don't know what to say. My future? Do I really have one? I really want to go to sleep.

"You wouldn't want to marry a famous man? A footballer like me?"

A husband? And why not children? I never imagined that I would leave this house alive. From there to imagining that I could lead a normal life, meet a boy and start a family...

"I could help you," he adds, "introduce you to boys. But for that, you have to do something for me."

Just then, I see his hand disappear into his pants. A wave of disgust sweeps over me, I can see what he is doing. I step back.

"What do you want?" I ask.

"To play with you! You'll see."

"What does that mean?"

"That I want to sleep with you!"

"No!"

I want to scream, but Godwin doesn't give me the chance. A powerful hand grabs my throat. Suffocating, gasping, I cry, I beg. I tell him that he can have all the girls he wants, that he should leave me alone. I tell him that if Linda finds out, she'll go crazy... None of my arguments seem to touch him. I fight with the energy of desperation. In vain. He spreads my legs with force. I was taken from my family! I was deprived of my childhood! I was robbed of school, of an education, of a future! I do not want to fall any lower. I push him back. I twist in all directions to try to escape his hold, but what can I do against a man of his strength? He lies down on me, crushing me with his weight. Suddenly, the pain. Searing. Harrowing. Burning. How long does this disgrace last? How much time does my innocence take to die? I don't know. My mind is cut off from my body. I have the impression I will lose consciousness but I don't…

Then Godwin gets up. In the space of a second, I see his eyes. He is empty. I read neither remorse nor hatred. Not even the satisfaction of having fulfilled his disgraceful need. Nothingness. At the moment that I get up, he pinches my cheek with his fingers. Not like a father teases his daughter. Not to play. To hurt. He squeezes hard and, with his other hand, blocks my throat.

"If I want, I can make your life hell," he snarls. "So, you don't say anything to anyone…"

I can feel the pressure of his hand strangling me.

"If you talk, I'll kill you!" he says before disappearing.

I remain there, alone, under the raw beam of the light bulb. I am broken. Speechless. Dirty. Little by little my tears dry up. I don't move any more. I don't think any more. My body is not suffering. Much less than my head, at any rate. Violent feelings of an intensity that I had never known before invade me. Hate. Disgust. Godwin Okpara adopted me, he promised me that I would go to school. He lied. I have become a slave in his house. The public goes to the stadium and pays to see him play football. He's a star that goes on TV. People admire him! People love him! Only I know who Godwin Okpara really is: a bastard, a rapist!

I cannot denounce him. I cannot even complain. To whom could I go and seek help? Linda? She would poke my eyes out, rip out my tongue! Mamie? That would be the same, since she would tell Linda…

I get up and head towards my box. I take my little notebook out to confide my suffering and despair to it alone.

Then I go back to sleep on my mattress. I curl up in a ball, like a baby in the belly of its mother. My tears fall again, vinegar tears that burn my eyes. I would like the pain to stop. I would like the tears to stop falling. I would like everything to stop… even my life.

8

"You are ugly!"

"Papa" has become too heavy a word. After what happened, I am unable to say it. Each time I run into Godwin in the house, I think about what he did to me. I feel the wound in my flesh and in my heart. He lied to me. He betrayed me. He never had the slightest intention of putting me in school, of offering me a better life, as he told my father. From the beginning, it was planned that I would be their slave. He watched me grow up, waiting for the day that he could use me to satisfy his urges. I live now in the fear of him attacking me again. I live now between the terror that Linda inspires in me, as she has come back, and the fear of finding myself face-to-face with Godwin. Luckily, most of the time he stays in Belgium.

Days, weeks and months pass without him assaulting me again. Summer comes. A burning hot summer, like in Africa. But here in France the heat wave has led to tremendous devastation and the television shows terrible images. Hundreds and hundreds of elderly people succumb to the high temperatures. The Chemin des Petits-Chênes villa is overwhelmed by the heat. In my cellar, there is a sickening mugginess. I am, however, too tired not to go to sleep as soon as I lie down on my mattress.

Then it is the new school year. This time without Sophie. She was not granted permission to pass on to the next year because her school results were too poor. Linda had a fit of hysterics, yelled at the director of the international school, then had Sophie placed in a boarding school in London. For me, it is one less bed to make in the morning and less laundry to do, but I miss her in spite of it all.

Christmas is coming. Everywhere on the planet, people prepare to celebrate the birth of the Son of God, to speak of peace and love, solidarity and brotherhood. Children go to sleep dreaming of the man in the red suit who is going to bring them presents. It has been a long time since I have had those dreams. I remember my last Christmas in Nigeria at my Uncle Bala's house after my mother's death. That day, he allowed me to wear a pretty dress. Since I have been in France, Christmas no longer means anything.

And yet, this time, the holidays are making me happy. I am working with gusto. For a time, Linda's blows and insults no longer hurt and I feel like singing because I heard Linda on the telephone: Magda, Patrick and their children are coming to spend the holidays with us!

I am crazy with happiness at the idea of seeing them again, but when their car pulls up in front of the house, I suddenly feel fear in my heart. I could not go out to meet them. I have the impression that a blemish is inscribed on my forehead, in my eyes. I am afraid that when she takes me in her arms, when I feel her lips on my cheek, that Magda will read me like an open book and discover all this filth. I must not break down! I cannot collapse at her feet. Luckily, Steeve, Sandy and Samuel arrive and make a joyful party for our guests. That turns everyone's attention away and allows me to lift my spirits. I hold up well. I say nothing to Magda. This first moment has passed, I now know that I will manage to keep the secret deep inside me.

As usual, in Magda's presence, my lot improves.

A few days before Christmas, Magda and Mamie have gone out. Linda calls me. I join her in the kitchen. She wants me to peel vegetables.

"And I encourage you not to be slow!" she grumbles.

She leaves me there and goes upstairs. I hear the sound of her feet on the stairs then the sound of the television in the children's living room. That means that she is lying on the couch and it will not take long before she is snoring like a lumberjack.

Godwin arrives a few moments later. He stands at the doorway for a moment without saying anything. His look, on my shoulders, weighs a ton. I concentrate on my work without lifting my head. He comes into the room, stands in front of the stove.

"We have to go and buy some gas," he suddenly says.

I look at him, incredulous. What has taken hold of him to take care of the kitchen at this hour? How suspicious!

"Gas? But the cylinder was changed two days ago!"

He knows very well that we always have a spare bottle.

"Exactly! We have to replace the empty bottle."

"Magda went this morning and was told that there would be no gas for two or three days."

It is past seven o'clock in the evening. It is dark outside. Godwin insists. My intuition is shouting at me that a trap is being set.

"Mama told me to prepare the vegetables. She is going to be furious if I don't obey."

"She's sleeping. You'll finish later."

I wipe my hands on the dish towel and obey. I don't have a choice. I load the empty bottle in the back of the four-by-four. I close the back and get into the car. When Linda drives, I am not allowed to sit up front. She claims that I smell so bad that my odour seeps into the seats. Godwin tolerates me by his side. He arrives and gets in behind the steering wheel without a word. The four-by-four starts and we drive towards Le Vésinet.

We soon stop at a service station where the salesman confirms that the gas is out of stock. He tells us to come back in two or three days, but Godwin starts the car saying we'll go look elsewhere. More and more convinced that he is preparing a dirty trick, I press myself against the door, as if to keep myself as far away from him as possible.

We keep going a bit longer into the night. Through the windows, I try to get my bearings, to guess where we are and where we are going. My heart starts to panic. I would so much like to recognize the way home. Suddenly, the headlights shine onto a signpost. It indicates that we are going towards Paris. That means that we are turning our back to the house. I think of Linda…what is going to happen when she wakes up and finds out that I abandoned my post? I will have a hard time explaining that I only obeyed Godwin. She will fly into a rage and take it out on me. My only hope is that Magda is nearby at that moment and that her protection saves me from a thrashing. Little by little, as the car moves on in the night, I feel fear wrapping around me, twisting into me. The fear invades me, taking possession of my mind. I fight to avoid panicking. Is it a dream or have we turned around? Are we really heading back towards the house? I don't dare hope…

"It is late and Mama wants me to prepare the vegetables," I say to break the silence.

Godwin says nothing or, rather, he waits a long moment before answering.

"We are going to go back, don't worry."

Why do these words not reassure me? Why do they give me the urge to scream with terror? My nerves are on end, as if they are being rubbed with sandpaper. And yet, outside, I start to recognize some elements of the landscape. An intersection, a turn. Yes! We are heading back towards Chatou! I'm saved!

Having arrived in sight of a rest stop, Godwin slows down, turns on his turn signal and puts the four-by-four into the parking area. Two trucks, like two sleeping mastodons, are parked there. Godwin slides his four-by-four between the two vehicles, then turns off the engine. All of a sudden, the headlights are off. The night swallows us.

"Get in the back!" Godwin growls.

My heart is beating strongly. I'm scared! My God, you cannot know how scared I am!

"Get in the back, I said!" Godwin repeats. "We'll do this quickly and then we'll go home."

The memory of the burning comes back to my mind. It bores into my brain! It spreads throughout my body. I don't want that to start again.

I scream, "No!"

"Get in the back!" he repeats.

Anger twists his mouth into an awful snarl. His eyes shoot lightning. I nevertheless meet his look full of threat. For just one second, I think about the situation. Linda is at home and eventually Magda and Patrick will be too. He will never dare make a scandal in front of them. So I open the door, rush outside and run straight ahead. Luckily, I manage to understand where we are and I go in the direction of the house.

I march on with determination. He won't touch me. My feet hit the asphalt with the rhythm of my heart beat. I press on. And on.

Every step separates me a little more from a new torture session.

Behind me, I hear the sound of a door slamming. The engine starts. Godwin manoeuvres the four-by-four between the trucks. I don't run nor do I hurry up when I hear the car approaching. I continue walking straight ahead. The light from the headlights brightens my back, my shoulders, then catches on a shadow at my feet and stretches it out to a never-ending horizon. The car passes right in front of me without slowing down. I just have the time to see Godwin's silhouette behind the steering wheel. I follow the four-by-four with my eyes as it disappears. I remain alone in the night, in the cold, walking resolutely towards the house.

I try to imagine the coming events.

Do they wonder where I am? Are they looking for me? Will Linda ask Godwin if he has seen me? And in that case, what will he answer? In my head, the ideas and questions buzz like a swarm of bees. I have never told anyone what happened in the cellar the night that Godwin came down after the fight with his wife. I have dug a trench, a deep tomb in my heart and I have hidden this horrendous secret there. I cried, alone, on my mattress, for the funeral of my innocence and my childhood. I cursed him, he who lied to me, betrayed me, dirtied me, but I have said nothing. To anyone. Ever.

I arrive at the house, chilled to the bone. I am so cold that I feel like my skin has turned blue. My heart leaps into my throat when I see Linda and Mamie on the front step. They see me too. They are waiting for me!

I come up to the house, trying to decode the feelings written on Linda's face. Her look is as hard as stone, her features are as frozen as those of a statue. At her sides, just as impassive, is Mamie who is standing with her arms crossed.

"Where were you? Why are you coming home on foot?" The tone is dry. Broken. Her words fire and explode like the bullets of a revolver.

"Getting some gas," I stammer.

Linda looks at me for a moment. Then she turns around and heads towards the garden.

"Come this way," she growls.

I follow her with Mamie on my heels to the glass door of the guest room which is open and Linda goes into the house. In one second, I understand. She wants to interrogate me, but without Magda or Patrick hearing or seeing anything. That's why we have to avoid the front door. We are now all three in this room. Linda closes the glass door…

"Why are you coming home on foot?" she hisses again.

I feel like a criminal in front of my judges. I am the one who is suspected and interrogated, while I am the victim. This time, it is too much. She wants to know? Well, here is the whole story! In a few sentences, I tell her everything. The kitchen where I am peeling the vegetables. Godwin who intended to go and get some gas. I say clearly that I refused. Oh, it is not easy to tell this. I am shivering with fear, I drown my words with tears. But I continue somehow. I explain that the car was parked between the trucks. And the rest. All the rest!

"What are you talking about?" Linda shouts. Her eyes are jumping out of her head. I step backwards. And I start again.

"He said to me: 'We'll do this quickly and we'll go home.'"

"What does that mean, 'We'll do this quickly'? Fuck! What does that mean?"

The guest room disappears all of a sudden. I feel as if I am thrown aside by a tornado, a flood, a crazy river. I try to fight with all my strength against the current, to swim, to survive. Every word that comes out of my mouth risks being my last. In front of me, Linda is like a bomb at risk of exploding at any moment.

"I don't know what that means… but I was scared. That's why I left on foot."

Pitiful explanations. The terror that Linda inspires in me forbids me from telling the truth.

"I don't know, I don't know…"

That's all I am able to keep repeating.

"Liar!" she screams. "Who do you take me for? You think that my husband wants to sleep with you? Is that what you think?"

I hunch up, ready to cover my head with my arms before the hail of blows falls on my skull. She screams even louder, sputtering left, right and centre.

"You think that, huh? Bitch! You think you're beautiful?"

I don't dare reply.

"I asked you if you think you're beautiful?"

"No!"

"My husband is a footballer!" she yells. "He can have all the women he wants! All the women, you understand! And you think that he wants to sleep with you? With an animal that stinks?"

What could I say? None of my words would carry any weight. At any rate, the door opens and Godwin Okpara appears, the man who can have all the women he desires but who raped his adopted daughter in his cellar.

"You know what she is saying?" his wife asks him. "She says that you wanted to sleep with her."

Godwin knits his brows, pulling a face that is at once disgusted and indignant. Hypocrite!

"It is true that I told her to get in the back," he acknowledges. "But it is because she got into the front. I was reminding her where her place is!"

Linda screams again. Insults. Dirty words. But I don't hear anything any more. I don't even know what I think. Suddenly, I realize that Godwin has left the room. Mamie looks at me gravely. Linda shakes me by the arm.

"You have wronged your father!" She screams to me. "Go and apologize."

At times, even when the injustice is too much, one dares not say a word, one does not even have the courage to protest. You live each second hoping that everything will stop. It is while wishing with each one of my steps that lightning will strike me down and make me disappear forever that I go into the living room. Godwin is waiting, sitting on the couch. I kneel down in front of him, my head down.

"Papa, I ask your forgiveness."

My heart is torn. I cry. Is it possible to still have so much sorrow inside? I have already cried so much…

———

Magda and her daughter come to find me later in the evening. They heard the shouts and guessed that something had happened. Magda takes my hand in hers. I feel her warmth.

I look into her eyes and I see a great worry. Great sadness too.

"Tina," she begins, "what is happening here?"

"Nothing."

"Tell me everything! Tell me everything!" she begs.

I hesitate a moment. Linda did not believe me. Is Magda going to believe me? She has known Godwin for so long. They are friends. She knows that he is a man who loves women, pretty women. After the games he goes to party with girls. Could she believe that he wants to sleep with me? With Tina, the ugly girl? Tina, the stupid girl? Tina who stinks?

I explain the gas cylinder episode in a few words. Magda holds me against her and kisses me on the forehead. At this moment, Linda calls me and our conversation ends. Unfortunately, I will not have the occasion to see Magda again alone.

On Christmas evening, a surprise is waiting for me under the tree. There is an envelope with my name on it. I open it trembling and discover a fifty-euro note. Even more surprising is that it wasn't Magda who put this with the presents. It was Linda herself. It is so unexpected and it doesn't seem like her. I don't delude myself, it is to the presence of Magda that I owe this gift and it is her that I thank in my heart.

A few days later, Magda, Patrick and their children have returned to Belgium. Linda sends me out to go shopping at the supermarket.

"You can pay with the Christmas note," she tells me.

Nothing will ever change for me in this house of nightmares. Nothing! Yes, something. One detail, but one that has enormous importance for me. Mamie came to see me in the cellar, she put her wrinkled face in front of mine and she said:

"I believe you. About Godwin... I believe you."

9

Running away

"Tina! Come here! Right now!"

When Linda calls me with this tone of voice, I had better arrive forthwith. I put down the iron and rush into the living room where she is waiting for me with a pair of scissors in her hand. She catches me by the arm and turns me around forcibly.

"Too long! Disgusting!"

She is talking about my hair. I am used to it. I know what I have to do. I kneel down in front of her. With a disgusted face, she forces the blades into the shapeless mass of my hair and cuts and hacks. Clip, clip, clip. I see the hair fall on the ground. In less than two minutes, the affair is over and my head resembles nothing. Spikes stick out in all directions, some parts are longer than others and here and there, holes let my scalp show through. I stand up in tears, my head lowered, and go back to my ironing.

"Thank you Mama," I say, leaving the room.

I feel humiliated, put down, crushed by shame and sorrow. If only being made ugly by Linda would keep her husband away from me. Alas! It is not the case. Because, of course, he has come back to the cellar. I defended myself.

I tried to escape him. He hit me. And he started again, in spite of my cries, in spite of my tears.

My ordeal has since become daily because, at the end of the 2004 football season, the Liège team thanked Godwin and now, there is no more club. Linda, who manages his career, sees the opportunity to negotiate a new transfer, a new contract. She plans on sending her husband to Dubai, where a footballer can earn a lot of money… In the meantime, Godwin trains at home and every time he finds himself alone with me he makes the most of it, several times per day even, so often that I can no longer say how many times.

I can't handle it any more. If I don't run away, I am going to die. But I know that I don't have the right to make a mistake. If I run away and they catch me, they will send me back to Nigeria where they have "friends" and where they can buy anything with their money.

At the beginning of the summer, my plan to run away is ready. I only have to wait for the opportunity. Finally the day I have been so hoping for has arrived! Tuesday, 13 July 2004. Linda calls me. I run and find her ready to leave at the front door. She gives me a twenty-euro note.

"For the shopping!" she bellows in a bad mood.

Then she leaves. When Linda goes out, I have the feeling that even the house breathes a sigh of relief. But even during her absence, her hold remains and there is still a strange atmosphere. The fear that she induces in us has set us one against another. No one trusts anyone else. Everyone acts as a guard against the other. Each one is saving their own skin. And mine is worth less than that of the others.

I start by checking on where the others are. Godwin has gone out running. While waiting to find a club, he stays in shape by running regularly. Mamie is watching television in the living room and the children are in their rooms. I go down to the cellar and put my things into a small sports bag. I remain a minute looking at my luggage. I am going to leave here! Go far away! They will never find me! I have a hard time believing it. What do I need on the run? I need my passport. I know where my papers are since I am the one who puts all the things away in the house. Then I remember the photos that were taken away from me, the portraits of my parents. I go up into Mamie's room and open her wardrobe. My heart is beating hard, but if someone surprises me going through her affairs I have planned to say that I had forgotten to put something away. I find my precious photos in the same spot where I left them the last time. Quickly, I hide them under my T-shirt and go back downstairs furtively to get a rubbish bag in the kitchen. Back in the cellar, I put the photos away in the sports bag that I place inside the rubbish bag.

A few moments later, I drop off the bag on the pavement in front of the house, as if it were the household rubbish. Finally, I go back to my work, as if nothing is happening. I make great efforts to appear normal. I'm afraid that my face betrays me, that a gesture accomplished too quickly or one word too much would awake suspicions.

Then I look for Mamie.

"I'm going out to do the shopping," I tell her. "Mama asked me to."

She does not reply. At the moment I step out of the house, I fear that she will call me or that an old wrinkled hand will grab me on the shoulder and hold me back. But none of that happens.

It is so easy I have a hard time believing it. A look to the left, a glance to the right and no one is on the horizon so I open the rubbish bag to get out my things. Without waiting a second, I head towards the train station. Each step takes me further from the house. Each step brings me closer to freedom.

Here I am at the train station. I look at the signs. My glance stops on a name. Meaux. Where is that? I don't have any idea, but I head to the ticket office and ask for a ticket to this destination. Imitating the other travellers, I validate my ticket and take my seat in the train. I sit next to a window, my sports bag on my knees.

Finally, the doors of the train close and we start speeding up. All around me in the wagon, people read and talk… others sleep. For them, this is an ordinary, humdrum trip. For me, this is the great escape!

The train rolls along and cradles my dreams of freedom with its rocking movements. Through the window I see the landscape passing by, and the houses, the roads, the people. A real spectacle, the most beautiful I have ever seen! The train makes several stops. Travellers disembark. Others get on and take their seats.

The Meaux train station, where I finally get off the train, empties in just a few minutes. I remain there, alone and lost, with my sports bag under my arms. I sit down on a bench for a while to get my bearings. The air that I am breathing threatens to explode my lungs. I have the impression of being far from the villa in Chatou. At the other end of the world. I do not know that I am only sixty kilometres away, not even an hour by car. What are they doing over there? I imagine them looking for me. Perhaps they have gone down to the cellar and discovered that I have disappeared. Linda screams and curses me. She cuts through the wind with her big arms and threatens to break all my bones when I come back. But I will not go back. I have a firm resolution.

Time goes on and little by little I understand that I am at a dead end. I cannot stay here in the train station without appearing suspicious. Young people, hanging about the area, throw me sidelong glances. They must find me strange with my clothes from another era and my shaved head.

At regular intervals, a train stops and lets off more travellers. I watch the human flow rushing out of the train station. What if I asked for help from one of these women?

Instinctively, I speak to women of colour. Naively, I tell myself that they will be more likely to help me because of the colour of my skin. A few go right by in front of me without even looking at me when I speak to them. Others don't understand a thing from my gibberish and move away quickly. One of them stops, finally. I explain that I am lost, that I have nowhere to go.

"But what are you doing here by yourself?" she asks, astonished.

"I ran away because my parents abuse me…"

Her eyes look away from mine.

"I cannot help you," she tells me. "I live alone with my daughter. It is too small at my place. Really, I cannot house you there."

She moves away quickly, without turning back, repeating, "I cannot, I cannot…" as if she was trying to convince herself. I quickly understand that no one will come to my aid. All the same, I am not panicking. I feel calm, peaceful and free. I leave to walk around the town. Everything is new to me. The merest window is a spectacle. I start to feel tired and my bag feels heavier and heavier. My steps bring me back to the train station without my really noticing and I sit down under a bus shelter. The sky seems to be getting darker. Night is not going to be long in coming. I envision sleeping in the train station, on a bench. It seems the best solution.

A car comes up to me and slows down. The driver, a young guy, stops at my level and leaves the engine running.

"Hello," he says, "you've been here for a while…"

I have to find something to tell this boy. Quickly! The problem is that although I understand French more or less, I don't speak it terribly well. I try to invent a story, mixing English and the few words of French that I have learned over time.

"I wanted to surprise a friend," I explain to him as well as I can, "but she is not home so I am all alone…"

Is he going to believe my lie? Does he even understand what I'm saying? I would like him to go off in his car again and not cause me any trouble.

"If you stay here, you are going to end up having problems," he tells me.

"Problems?"

"Cops. They will take you away."

Police! Definitely not. The boy seems to think for a moment and then he says:

"I can't give you a place to stay, but I can take you to my friend's house."

I weigh up the pros and the cons. Leaving with a stranger to sleep at another stranger's house is not reassuring. But, on the other hand, this boy is surely right about the police and I have no desire to be arrested on my first day of freedom!

I get up and the boy leans over to open the door.

"My name is Kevin," he says, restarting the car.

A few moments later, he parks in front of a small building. I follow him to the friend's flat. When Kevin explains my situation to him, he accepts having me over for the night.

Though tiny, with just a corridor, a kitchen in the corner and one room, the flat is apparently used to greet squatters travelling by like me. In a cupboard cleverly devoid of its shelves, a mattress has been placed on the ground. A guest room of two square metres!

The three of us have a meal together. I have eaten nothing since that morning but even so, I am not very hungry. I eat a sandwich nevertheless. Kevin's friend speaks English, almost as well as I speak French. By mixing the two languages and making a lot of gestures, I perform a small miracle—that of holding a real discussion until late in the night. Kevin seems kinder and kinder to me. His friend gets out some tobacco and rolling papers and makes a cigarette. When he lights it, a strong odour fills the room. He inhales two or three puffs before offering his cigarette, between his index finger and thumb, to Kevin who inhales a breath in turn, closing his eyes in ease.

"You want some?" he asks me.

I decline the offer. I have never smoked even tobacco, so you can imagine what marijuana would do to me!

We talk some more. Outside, night has fallen. The strong odour of marijuana fills the room, a smell that goes to the head. Kevin and his friend make me understand that they haven't been fooled, they don't believe one word of my story. I protest calmly and repeat that it is true. These two boys must have the habit of keeping secrets, because they don't try to find out more. It is late when we go to bed, Kevin and his friend sleep in the room and I stay in the converted closet. Soon I hear the regular breathing of my hosts sleeping peacefully.

On my side, in spite of the crushing fatigue, I have a hard time going to sleep. As soon as I close my eyelids, I see Godwin and Linda. Mamie as well. In my nightmare, they are gigantic. They stride over cities and fields. They are looking for me. Stubbornly. Furiously. I know they have not told the police because they want to capture me themselves and punish me in their way. I hear them! They are coming… they are right behind the door!

10

At the police station

I wake up the next morning as tired as the night before. The nightmares of the dark hours exhausted me. I eat and have a bowl of coffee in the company of Kevin and his friend. I don't know why, but the desire to finally tell them at least part of the truth comes to me. It is complicated because my bad French breaks the story up and makes it difficult to follow. Nevertheless, they listen with patience to the summary of my miserable existence. I explain to them that I live with my adoptive parents. I tell them that I was brought over from Nigeria after the death of my mother as they promised my father that I would get a real education… but, in reality, I have never been to school. I tell them that I sleep in a cellar and that I have to do all the work in the house.

"In reality, you are their slave!" Kevin announces. "That's awful!"

His indignation appears sincere and he and his friend ask me a thousand questions. What time do I get up? Five o'clock! What time do I go to bed? When my adoptive mother wants me to. What do I do all day? I iron, I do the washing, I cook… I take care of the house. I massage the feet of my mistress and flush the toilet when she has relieved herself.

"And your father?" Kevin asks.

Silence. The words stay in my mouth, the secret at the depths of my heart.

"He doesn't care. He's a bastard."

"You have to get out of their house," Kevin concludes.

That's what I'm doing, but where can I go now? I have no family, no friends. No one. I cannot keep sleeping in his friend's cupboard.

"There is an emergency number for abused children," Kevin says. "I saw it on television. You can call from any phone booth."

All three of us leave a few moments later for the nearest phone booth. Kevin was right. An announcement says that there is a service operating twenty-four hours a day and seven days a week for abused children. All I have to do is to walk into the phone booth, pick up the phone and dial three digits, 119, to be saved. The end of all of these misfortunes is here, at my fingertips. Nevertheless, I don't make the slightest move. What good can it do to pick up the phone? Why dial this number? I know that the person at the other end of the line will not understand what I'm saying. There is no prison more solid for me than the language barrier. Linda and Godwin knew very well what they were doing preventing me from learning French.

Kevin understands my problem. He comes into the phone booth too.

"You want me to call?" he asks, not waiting for my reply. I hold my breath when I see his finger on the numbers.

"I am with a young girl who has a problem," he explains. "It's an emergency."

He listens, repeats the directions someone has explained to him on the other end of the line; then moves closer. A smile lights up his face.

"I have an address," he announces triumphantly. "A centre where they will take care of you."

Saved! This boy that the heavens placed on my path is saving my life! We get back into the car and start off. We stop a few minutes later in front of a modern, soulless building.

Kevin takes me right up to the door.

"There you go. Here we will go our separate ways. But I will call here tomorrow to hear how things are going."

I thank him again and I go into the building. At the reception desk, I am told that someone is going to meet me. The name is told to me without my being able to remember it. A woman finally arrives and, with a big smile, asks me to follow her. We enter an office and the woman asks me to sit down.

I can barely look at her. I notice her skirt and her high heels. She is a very elegant woman and her voice is soft. She asks me questions and notes my answers. My first name. My last name. Where I come from. What I have lived through. When I tell her the details of my ordeal, a sad shadow passes over her face. She suffers for me, with me. Suddenly, she picks up her pen from the pad of paper as if a fly has just bitten her.

"I forgot to ask you your age," she says.

"I am sixteen years old," I answer.

Her appearance suddenly changes entirely. She looks at me with fright, as if I have just made the coarsest of remarks.

"No, no, no, no, no, no!" she exclaims.

She sounds like a machine-gun. She puts down her pen and moves her hands about. I don't understand what is happening. I am afraid. I would like her to stop saying "No, no, no, no, no!" and for her to stay seated and not go away from me towards the door.

She opens the door and at the moment she crosses the threshold, she turns to me looking very disturbed as if she can now see my dirty clothes, my eyes swollen with fatigue and sorrow and my shaved head.

"This is a centre for adults!" she finally says.

She points a finger in my direction.

"Don't move! Stay there, I'm going to call…."

"Not my parents! I don't want to go back home to my parents!"

"No, not your parents…"

I weep.

"Not home…"

"Calm down, Mademoiselle," she says. "I am going to find someone who can help you."

After a moment of panic, I am reassured. The unexpected change in attitude of this woman terrifies me, but everything is going to be okay. I am going to be entrusted to the right person to take care of my case. Everything will be okay. I don't know how long I remain on my chair, waiting, thinking of my adoptive parents who, this time, have definitely understood that I am gone. I ask myself if they have gone to the police to register my disappearance. It seems improbable to me, then impossible. When there is something to blame oneself for, we don't go to the police. It would be like leaping into the wolf's mouth.

Suddenly, the office door opens and the woman reappears.

"There she is," she says.

She opens the door to let two men come in. Two men in navy blue uniforms! Policemen!

The police car takes us directly to the police station. Once there, the law enforcement officers indicate a bench for me to sit on. Around me, men and women in uniforms and civilian clothes, come and go, calling out to one another… There is a lot of activity, but no one attends to me. I remain on the bench with my bag on my knees. Then two men in plain clothes come to see me and ask me to follow them. They take me to a small office.

"What is your name?" one of them asks me.

My mouth remains closed.

"Have you run away?" the other policeman asks.

"My parents abuse me, so I left…"

"Who are you parents? Where do you live?"

"Chatou. They are not my real parents."

I notice their annoyance from their way of asking questions. These two men have less patience than Kevin to try and understand what I am saying. They don't have time to lose with a young runaway who is poorly dressed and dirty. Can't they see that I am an abused young girl? Is it not written on my face, in my eyes full of tears?

"Tell us your name or this is going to end badly," one of them repeats coarsely.

I am not moved. These police officers, after all, are much less terrifying than Linda. I imagine that if I tell them who I am and where I come from, they will send me back to the family. So, stubbornly, I refuse to reveal my identity to them.

Finally, the interrogation ends. The two policemen send me into the corridor and the waiting starts again. My head becomes heavier and heavier until I feel sleep carrying me away. I nod off, sitting on the bench in the corridor full of policemen.

How long did I sleep? Impossible to say. Sufficiently long, in any case, for a policeman to take my sports bag without my noticing. I leap up onto my feet seeing my opened bag and my affairs scattered about. They searched and found my passport! Through the open door, I see the two men who interrogated me earlier. One of them is holding my papers in his hand.

"Her name is Tina Okpara. We will have to see if there is a missing person report."

"Okpara," the other says, "like the football player from Paris Saint-German?"

"Yes, I would say so."

The policeman who took my passport sits down at a desk and types on a computer.

"Bingo!" he says. "Her family reported her running away yesterday."

He takes his time and adds: "And she is indeed the daughter of Godwin Okpara, the player from PSG!"

When they come back, I can see that their expressions have changed. They look hard at me now with curiosity. What is surprising to them at this point? That the daughter of a well-known footballer could be so poorly dressed? That I would want to run far away from a rich and famous father? Perhaps they are fans of Paris Saint-Germain? They watch the games on TV and read commentaries in *L'Équipe*, the national sports newspaper. They admire Godwin Okpara, his tackles, his dribbles… perhaps I should tell them what he does to me when he comes down to join me in the cellar!

I suddenly feel weary, exhausted. All my strength has been drained from my body and I succumb to fatigue, falling asleep right there on the bench.

"Come with us," one of the inspectors tells me, shaking me by the arm.

I get up and follow him along the corridor to the area where the cells are lined up. The policeman opens a door and asks me to enter a sordid, sombre and grimy cubbyhole with a bunk bed. It is uncomfortable, but I am so tired, so desperate, that I lie down and fall asleep almost immediately.

I stay in this cell for a long time, where all the drunkards, dealers and hooligans have spent time… right up until a very familiar voice wakes me from my sleep.

"Tina! My granddaughter! Oh, my poor little granddaughter!"

It is Mamie. I have never seen her in such a state. She is wringing her hands, snivelling. Liar! Cheat! She takes me into her arms and holds me tight, repeating my name and how happy and relieved she is to have found me. She was so scared that something bad would happen to me! Why did I give them such a fright? Oh, how relieved my parents are going to be!

Mamie explains to the policemen that my adoptive parents are out of the country on a trip. She is here to pick me up with a friend of the family, a fan of Godwin's more precisely. He met my adoptive father when he was out running and they got to know each other. He has been to the house two or three times and we have been to his house sometimes to have lunch with his family.

We leave the police station a few minutes later. Outside, I am surprised to see that it is dark. I have completely lost track of time. I am like an empty shell. I get into the car. We do not go back to Chatou. First, we have to go and pick up the children from Godwin's friend's house. When we arrive, it is too late to wake them up and we all spend the night there. At any rate, I am in no hurry to go back.

———————

The next morning, the house is deserted when we arrive. Everyone goes about their business, but you can feel that minds are elsewhere. It is as if the crew of a boat is preparing to encounter a storm. Hurricane Linda. I only think of her. Impossible to get her out of my thoughts! Fear gnaws away at my belly. Is she going to beat me? Surely, yes, there is no doubt. She is going to break a spatula on my head. She is going to scream, to yell, to insult me and to treat me like an animal. The day goes by in this way. I tremble at the slightest noise of a car engine approaching. I jump at the slightest sound. I am in the midst of putting away some linen in a room when a car hoots right in front of the house. It is as if an iron hand has reached into my chest and ripped out my heart. Doors slam. The front door opens and I hear the voices of Linda and Godwin. I guess that they have met Mamie in the living room. I hear voices without understanding exactly what they are saying. Then Mamie comes up to get me.

"Linda wants to see you," she tells me.

I go back down with her. Linda is sprawled in an armchair and Godwin is standing near the glass door. I don't dare to make the slightest gesture. I even have a hard time breathing.

Linda turns her pit bull face to me.

"Why did you run away?" she begins with a soft voice, as if she were trying to contain her anger.

I shake my head.

"Why did you run off?" she repeats.

"I don't know…"

"Are you badly treated here?"

"No."

"You don't eat your fill perhaps?"

"Yes I do…"

She continues. It is a rolling fire of questions. Is she unjust with me? Someone is nasty to me? Does she not do everything for me to be happy? And shouldn't I bless Godwin for having adopted me?

Each time, I answer yes, no, yes, no, I say what she wants me to.

"So, why did you leave the house?"

"The devil made me do it…"

It is the only explanation that comes to my mind. Suddenly, a barrage of shouting echoes in the room.

"You know what?" Linda screams. "It is not you who is going to fuck me up! It is not an animal who is going to fuck me up! Bitch! What do you think? That you are smarter than me?"

It lasts a century. The roaring fills my head, echoing in my skull. I cry.

"What is your father going to think if I tell him how you behave with us?" Linda shouts at the peak of her anger. "You think he'll be proud of you?"

The allusion to my real father strikes my heart like a poisoned arrow. Nothing would cause me greater pain than imagining that my behaviour would upset him. The idea that I could cause some grief to my father, in Lagos, and my mother, in heaven, is unbearable to me. So I promise everything she wants, to be calm, to not run away any more. I start, as Linda orders me, by getting down on my knees and, in tears, asking for forgiveness from my adoptive parents for the worries I have caused them.

11

The torture chamber

After the violent scenes, it is always the same thing. Linda sulks! She spends days and days not speaking to me. If she has something to tell me or to ask me, she goes through Mamie. "Tell Tina to do this…" or "Send Tina to do the shopping." And so on. That doesn't prevent her from slapping me on the head from time to time, preferably when I am least expecting it.

She also doesn't hesitate to insult me. I am stupid. I am ugly. I am an animal or worse. What hurts me the most is when she takes it out on my father, when she claims that Simon Omaku never loved me, that he got rid of me. The proof? Does he call to ask for my news? No, never! I am nothing but a millstone to him and he is very happy to be rid of me. How disappointed he would be if he knew how I behaved!

Thinking of my father makes my heart ache and thinking that there is just one atom of truth in the spiteful things that Linda says is torture. Since I don't want her to see me in tears, nor to show her that she has affected me, I go and cry by myself.

Godwin has not changed his attitude towards me, alas! When we are alone in the house, every time he wants to, he makes me go down into the cellar with him. For a long time, I fought, I struggled. I pushed him back with my arms. I pressed my legs shut. But he is always stronger, of course. So now, I say no. I refuse. I want him to know that I do not want to. But I no longer struggle physically. It serves no purpose since he has the upper hand. I found another system of defence. When he throws me onto my mattress, I go far away in my thoughts, far, far away. I cut my mind off from my body. I am a piece of dead wood. Empty. Hollow.

If he knew how much he disgusts me! When he lies on top of me, when he gets up and gets dressed! How much I hate him when he hands me a ten-euro bill. Ten euros! That's how much he thinks my ruined childhood is worth! What does he think? That I am selling my body like a prostitute? That he is compensating me with his money? At times it is even worse, he finds it sufficient to say: "I already paid you last time…"

Godwin rapes me whenever he feels like it and without taking any precautions… so much so that one day I go to find him and coldly announce that my period is two weeks late. If I thought that it would make him ill at ease, I'm wrong.

"I'll take you to the doctor," he says.

We get in the car and he takes me to the family doctor, the one who regularly treats Sophie, Steeve, Sandy and Samuel and whom I saw just once, during my first winter in France, for a case of bronchitis.

On the way, Godwin explains to me what I should say to justify my state. He follows me into the family doctor's office to check that I recite my lesson well.

"I had sex with my boyfriend and I think I am pregnant."

The doctor listens to my chest vaguely and writes a prescription for a pregnancy test. Godwin pays for the appointment and recommends to the doctor not to say anything to Linda.

"She wouldn't understand," he explains. "She is old school."

Godwin next takes me to a medical laboratory. They take some blood and Godwin asks for the results to be sent to the doctor.

"Definitely not to the house," he says.

A few days later, Godwin calls me from Belgium.

"I just got the call from the doctor," he says. "The test was negative. You are not pregnant. The doctor thinks that you are late because of stress. He also found you 'sad and tired'."

There it is. End of story. Godwin managed that well. Linda won't know anything. The rapes can continue.

I never smile any more. I am never happy. I have no more hope. Magda doesn't even come to spend a few days at the house any more. I think that, as with many others, Linda made her flee. Too many fights. Too much shouting. Too much violence. It is always that way. People come to us for a time then disappear. Their visits become less and less frequent until the day that they no longer come at all.

In Linda's eyes, Magda and Patrick were also wrong to be, above all, Godwin's friends. Since he told them the story of "Uncle" and about her infidelity, Linda makes them feel that they are no longer welcome under her roof.

I am more isolated, more entrapped than ever in the Chemin des Petits-Chênes villa.

This day of February 2005, Linda leaves the house announcing that she is going shopping at Chateau-Rouge. I know this big African market in Paris. I love its stalls that overflow onto the pavements with skewers of smoked fish, plantain, tropical fruit and fragrant spices. Stalls selling wrappers. Street hawkers selling charms. Beauty shops where women have braids and coloured beads done in their hair. It is full of women in multicoloured wrappers and boubous and smells that remind me of my country.

I would love to go along, even if I am the one that has to carry all the shopping. But, alas, I have some work to do. I have to repair a tap leaking in the bathroom. Linda leaves with Mamie. The children are at school. I stay alone in the house. Alone with Godwin. He is in his room while I am being the plumber upstairs. With a screwdriver in my hand, I am working hard under the sink. Suddenly, the voice of my adoptive father makes me jump.

"Tina. Come here!"

With fear in my belly, I obey and join him. Am I again going to transform myself into a dead tree? Am I again going to have to swallow my tears, my suffering and my disgust?

Alas, yes… I can see it in his crazy eyes, in his obsessed look. He asks me to follow him into Sophie and Sandy's room. The first thing I see upon entering the room is my mattress. The mattress I sleep upon every night that he has gone to get from the cellar, to rape me in his girls' room.

It is sordid. Awful. And it revolts me. I push him back when he tries to drag me onto the mattress. I protect myself, but, as usual, he is stronger than me. After an exhausting, futile struggle, he throws me onto the mattress. In a moment, he is on me. His penis torturing me, killing me a little more every time he plunges into me, but Godwin couldn't care less about my suffering and my tears. He thinks only of his own pleasure!

He doesn't hear the car stopping in front of the house. He doesn't hear the front door opening. No more than he hears the heels clicking on the stairs, approaching the door of the room left ajar. And all of a sudden Linda comes in. She throws herself on him, screeching like a witch. Her strength increased tenfold by her rage, she grabs him by the hair and pulls him violently backwards. Then she throws herself on me. Her hands are the claws of a bird of prey, her fingernails the claws of a tigress. She wants to poke out my eyes, rip off my face.

Her blows fall on me, while she shouts.

"Slut! Whore!"

Godwin intervenes. Linda pushes him back. I try to run. She blocks the way and the blows again fall on me. On my head, on my arms, on my body. Suddenly, it stops. Godwin has managed to grab her by the arms. She turns back to him in fury and then the two of them start to fight. She rips through the air with her arms. He catches them by the wrists and alters their course. They yell. In English! In several languages! Without waiting, I rush out of the room. I hurtle down the steps, across the living room and open the glass door.

Outside it is pouring with rain. I straighten my clothes, but I am barefoot. I go out into the garden, cross the lawn and I jump over to Maria's house to hide in her rabbit hutch. That's where she finds me and sends me on my way after having made me my rubbish bag raincoat. I walk around a bit, before running into a woman. The one who lets me into her home, worries about me and gives me a dry sweater.

From her house, I call home. Godwin claims that everything is in order. How is that possible? I tell myself that I need to run, far, very far. But where can I go? I think again about running away to Meaux, about ending up at the police station. And I remember the reaction of the police officers to Godwin Okpara, the football player from Paris Saint-Germain, a famous man. He will always be believed. Never me.

So I head back to the villa. When I arrive, Godwin opens the door for me. The house is deserted, silent. Linda has gone out again. I enter and get back to my daily activities. What else could I do? I was trained this way. Godwin follows me everywhere. Every step I take he is behind me. He surely wants to make sure I don't run away again.

Then Linda comes home with Mamie. The children, who she went to pick up at school, are with her. She sends them to play in the living room and forbids them to come out before they are called. Then she closes herself up with Godwin in their room.

I hear shouting. Sounds of fighting. Mamie asks me to follow her into her room.

"What happened, Tina?" she asks.

"I defended myself," I answered.

She looks at me severely and reprimands me as if I were the guilty one.

"How could you let yourself go? How could you do such a thing, sleep with the husband of your mother?"

However much I defend myself, she doesn't want to hear it and continues to believe that I am, at least partly, consenting. The voice of Linda ends our discussion. She calls Mamie from the bottom of the stairs.

"Stay here! Don't do anything else silly!" the old lady tells me before going down.

I am alone in the room. I hear the front door open and Godwin's car starting.

He's leaving! The coward! The bastard! If he stayed, if he admitted that he forced me, that would protect me. I would receive fewer blows. That's certain. I understand now that he set a trap for me. He said that everything was in order so that I would come back. He stayed behind me so that I wouldn't run away. And now that his wife is here, he abandons me. He leaves me alone. He is washing his hands of me.

"It's the end! It's the end!" These words echo in my head. I am going to die now. I am sure. It couldn't be any other way.

The door of the room opens and Mamie appears.

"Mama wants to see you in the kitchen," she tells me.

I go down with the old woman on my heels.

"On your knees!" Linda orders me when I enter the kitchen.

I obey, a horrible fear in my belly.

"Was that good? You liked that?" Linda asked me.

Silence.

"You are just a slut who likes sex!" she continues. "I am going to give you a lesson that you will not forget so soon. Each time you want to sleep with a man, you will remember me! I am going to mark you until the end of your days!"

With my eyes full of terror, I see her light the flame under a pot of hot pepper sauce. Then she serves herself a big glass of vodka that she swallows in one gulp.

"Go up to the girls' room! There where you had my husband!" she growls.

I get up. My legs tremble and I stagger up the stairs. Mamie follows me like a shadow. We enter and I beg her to come to my rescue.

"You have to calm her down," I say, while joining my hands in prayer. "It is not me! He forced me! It is him!"

Has she forgotten the day when I ran away to avoid being raped in the back of the four-by-four when she came to tell me "I believe you"?

"Let her do what she has to do," she replies drily. "Her anger has to pass…"

The door opens again and Linda appears. A cigarette hangs from the corner of her lips and she is still holding her glass as well as a bottle of vodka. She also has scissors in her hands.

"Strip!" she yells. "Take off your clothes, you slut!"

I'm cold. I'm scared. I get undressed while trembling. I'm afraid of the pain. I'm afraid of the suffering. I am so scared that I would like to die. Now. Right now. Quickly! Quickly! Quickly! So that everything will stop! I call for death with all my strength, with all my soul. Linda comes near me, draws on her cigarette and blows smoke into my face.

"Every time you get undressed in front of a man, he will ask you where your scars come from. Then you will remember me! Always!" she snarls.

Then she crushes her burning cigarette into my face.

"On your knees!" she yells.

I get down. She grabs the scissors and cuts into my hair with broad movements. The blades ricochet against my skull, cutting into the scalp. Locks of hair fall to the ground. And my tears too. I cry. I empty myself of all my strength, of my breath, of my life… with these tears of terror. There I sit, trembling, shaven, on my knees in the middle of my hair when she yells orders at Mamie:

"Watch over this whore! I'll be back."

Upon her return, she is holding an object that I recognize, that I have often used to treat the children. It is a plastic graduated syringe we use to give them antibiotic syrup. Linda has filled it up with a red, smoking liquid… the hot pepper sauce! She serves herself another glassful of vodka. Does she need to intoxicate herself to have the courage to torture me? Her hate, her rage and her insanity are not enough?

With a thump, she sends me sprawling onto the ground. Then she throws herself on me, screaming again… shouts, threats, insults. With horror I feel the syringe digging between my legs. Linda cries out in joy when she applies the piston to inject her venom. I scream in pain. My stomach burns! She slaps me with force and gets up, taking her glass and her bottle again.

While I writhe in pain on the ground, she serves herself another vodka. She comes close to me, with crazy eyes, drinks a glass of alcohol and throws the rest of her glass into my face. Suddenly she is again on top of me. I scream when I feel the contact of the bottle between my legs.

"You like that?" she screams. "Is it good like that?"

In one blunt movement, she introduces the bottle into my genitals and gives it a kick that makes my belly explode. The pain is searing, unbearable. Everything turns around me. Everything goes black. I fly into a night without stars and in this night, I see the lightning of a blade. A razor flashes in Linda's hand.

"I am going to mark you forever!" she screams.

She reminds me of the witch from a horror film. Twice, she puts the sharp blade on my vagina and twice she traces a deep line. The blood spurts and flows down my legs. I scream again.

Is it the sight of blood? Is she finished with me? Has she finally subjected me to everything that I deserve in her eyes? She gets up now, leaving me on the ground.

"I hope that you have understood this time," she says. She heads towards the door, turning around before leaving.

"I don't want to see any blood on my carpet," she says. "Clean all of that up!"

She disappears. I get up, the burning in my belly, the blood running down my thighs. I cup my hand over my vagina, as if I could stop the red flow with my fingers. Mamie is there and looks at me gravely.

"That should teach you a lesson," she says, before leaving.

I limp to the toilet. Every step sets off thousand shards of pain. I slump onto the toilet and stay there. Everything turns… My sight blurs. The colours go out, things disappear… Mama, I am going to die! Mama, I am coming to you…

I don't know how long I stayed there, in agony, on the toilet. I finally get up and go to the bathroom. Just a few metres away. With a superhuman effort, I finally arrive. I collapse on the tiles and remain there, gasping, incapable of making another movement. Under me, the blood flow eases. Mamie arrives with a pack of compresses and a bottle of disinfectant. Wordlessly, she cleans my wounds. Little by little, the blood finally stops flowing. But the burning is still harsh. I can only walk with my legs very far apart.

I go down into the kitchen where I fill a bucket with water. I add bleach and go back up to the room to clean the traces left by my torture session. It is my blood, my own blood that I have to clean up.

12

Freedom!

The wounds take a long time to heal. And the healing is painful. It burns when I walk, it burns when I sit down, it burns when I go to bed… and it is worse yet when I go to the toilet. The pain is so intense that I almost faint every time I have to urinate. Two or three times, Mamie came to help me disinfect my wounds, then she left me a bottle of Betadine antiseptic and told me to do it myself.

Linda is sulking even more than usual. She does not speak to me and I have to leave the room if she comes in. She does not want to breathe the same air as me, she says.

Mamie suggests that I write an apology letter. She thinks that will diminish her anger. I think, above all, that Linda herself sent her to tell me to write this letter. Whatever the case, I take a piece of paper, a pencil and I write:

"I am very sorry, Mama. It will never happen again. I promise you that if it happens again, or if someone tells you that it has happened, you can do what you like with me. I promise you also that I will never run away again and that I will no longer lie and disobey Grandmother. I will be respectful, Mama. I am ready to follow your rules and to do what you want. I promise you that I will no longer betray you, Mama."

I sign it, "Tina."

Mamie takes the message to Linda. In response, she tells me that I must not speak to anyone of what she did to me, not even to my adoptive father. If ever she learns that I have complained, that I have spoken to someone, she will send me back to Nigeria. Over there, they will take care of me. Her friends. I imagine killers, men ready for anything. And I'm scared.

I live in the dread that Godwin will attack me again. I will do everything so that I am never, never again in the house alone with him.

With luck, weeks pass and Godwin doesn't come near me. I start believing that the fact of having been caught red-handed by his wife has calmed him for good. For months, not the slightest gesture, not a single look. Up until Saturday, 13 August 2005. This day will stay forever engraved in my memory.

I am in the house, working. Outside a bright sun is flooding the garden. Everything is calm. Not a sound.

Suddenly, I give a start. Someone is calling my name.

"Tina!"

It is Godwin's voice. I recognize the tone of his voice, the nuance. This is how he calls me when he wants me to go down with him to the cellar. I am crucified. Nailed to the spot. How could I believe that this man would one day leave me alone? It is impossible! This is evil. He is the devil. He made me think that he wanted to adopt me to make me happy, to give me a better future and he never sent me to school. He made me think that he loved me like a father and he raped me! He used his authority, his fame to trap me. And when he was found out, he lied again. He told me that everything was in order while he only wanted me to come home and he delivered me to the tigresses!

"Tina! Don't you hear me when I call you?"

The massive silhouette of Godwin stands out in the doorway. He has his bad look. His vicious look. I clench my fists.

"One day, you will regret it," I say.

It is not courage that gives me the strength to look into his eyes and to say these words, but desperation! Because I know that if he starts to rape me again, his wife will learn one day or another. And it is me, again, who will pay for it, me that she will torture! God alone knows if I could survive another session… I cannot even tell Godwin what she did to me after her last attack. Linda would send me to Nigeria to be killed. So, dead and done for either way, I spit the truth into his face.

Yes, me, Tina the slut, Tina the slave, Tina the animal, just good enough to do the housework, to flush the toilet when one has relieved oneself, just good enough to spread my legs when there are no other girls around, I put my face in his and I say to him:

"You will regret it! Today, I am small. I am nothing. It is easy for you to hurt me. But one day, you will run into me in the street and that day you will be ashamed. Ashamed of everything you did to me!"

"Who do you think you are?" he threatens. "I can kill you if I want…"

"You will be arrested and you will go to prison!"

"Not at all! I told Linda that I was going running and everyone thinks that I am in the forest jogging. They will find your body and they will blame a robber. I am well known. I am a football player. No one will think to suspect me…"

The slap he gives me almost takes my head off. My cheek is on fire and tears of rage flood my eyes. He stands there for a few seconds contemplating me with a threatening look. Suddenly, he turns on his heels and I see him disappear into the bathroom.

What is he going to do? Look for something? A mystery. I will never know, because at that very moment, without thinking, I run off. I race down the steps and through the living room. I find myself in the garden. Like the last time, I jump over the fence to land in Maria's property, but this time I am not going to hide in the tool shed. I go across her property in one go, without stopping, without turning around. Reaching the fence, I leap over again to land in another garden, then another. I am over fences and gates and I cross properties without stopping to catch my breath. I find myself on the road, almost without noticing. I look around me and I recognize the street where I spoke to the woman who gave me the white sweater. My brain is running full steam ahead. She told me to tell her if someone hurt me. Perhaps she is at home? I decide to try my luck.

———————

I am on the way when I see a young woman. I head towards her. She has curly blond hair.

"Madame, do you speak English?"

"Yes, a little. At least, I understand it…"

A glimmer of hope, finally! I decide to trust her and then I ask her the question that still haunts me forever.

"Do you know at what age a child can leave her family?"

"At eighteen," she answers. "Except in certain cases…"

She ends her sentence by shaking her hand above her head, to mime someone being hit.

"You mean, if someone is being abused?"

"Yes. If you are abused, if it is serious…"

I slowly nod my head. I garble a vague thank you and head off. Everything is suddenly jostling in my mind. I have the right to leave my family if I am abused. I have the right. But how can I do it? I haven't gone three metres when the young woman calls after me.

"Wait!"

I stop. The young woman joins me. She speaks calmly to me. She shows me a house not far from hers.

"The gentleman who lives there is a doctor," she says, still in English. "He is very kind and if asked, he can help you. Better than I can."

I hesitate.

"He can really help you," she insists.

The young woman tells me that her name is Nathalie and she asks me my name. I follow her to the doctor's house. We find him there with his wife in their garden in front of the house, pruning rosebushes. They are in the early years of their old age. They listen to Nathalie who explains the situation in a few words. She tells them that I am abused and looking for help. From time to time, she asks me a question in English and translates for the couple.

My tears have started to fall again. I know that I am pitiful in this rose garden, dressed in rags, hair cut anyhow. The eyes of this man and this woman who look at me from head to toe are like torture. What are they going to think of me?

"I feel that we cannot let this girl go away," the man says.

"We have to call the police!" his wife concludes.

I protest immediately.

"Not the police!"

The last time I dealt with the police, they sent me back to my family. I don't care if they arrest Linda and Godwin. All I want is to go far away from them. I just don't want to be abused any more, be raped no more. I want everything to stop. That's all. To be taken elsewhere. If these people have no other solution than calling the police, then I no longer have the faintest hope.

"I think I am going to go home. It's better," I say.

There is a long silence.

"I am going to give you my phone number," the wife of the doctor says. "You have to promise me to call if they hurt you. Okay?"

I accept and the woman goes inside to find something to write with. We wait. She takes a long time coming back. She finally arrives and gives me a piece of paper.

"You promise me," she insists. "If anyone hurts you…"

I repeat that I agree and I get ready to leave when she stops me.

"You come from Nigeria you say?"

"Yes, from Lagos."

"And these people who hurt you, they are not your real parents?"

"No, they adopted me."

"How old were you when you were adopted?"

"Twelve years old, Madame."

I don't understand what she is trying to find out. She asks me one question after another. She makes me repeat things that I had said earlier several times. Everything becomes clear when I hear the screeching of a siren.

"You've called the police!"

"Yes," she admits. "You must not be scared."

Not be scared? I feel I am being betrayed once again and I start to cry. Oh, these tears, will they never stop falling! Teni Omaku, did you bring me into the world for this? For tears and suffering?

"I don't want to! I don't want to!"

I shout with all my strength, but it is too late.

A car stops in the garden and three men in uniform get out. I am trapped. The doctor's wife invites us all to come inside the house. We will be more comfortable talking there. In the living room, I feel all alone in the midst of these strangers, some of whom carry revolvers. The doctor's wife asks me if I want to eat or drink something. I accept a glass of water.

"What is your name?" one of the policemen asks me.

I refuse to answer.

"We only know her first name," Nathalie explains. "Her name is Tina."

"We need to know your identity," the policeman explains. "We can't help you if we don't know who you are."

"I don't want to!"

It is all I can say, still in tears. One of the policemen, silent until then, comes up to me. He looks at me with a serious face.

"We are here for you," he tells me. "We are here to help you. It's our job and it's our responsibility. We will never let you return to the house of these people who hurt you. Never!"

Is it the tone of his voice? The determination I read in his eyes? This policeman and his two colleagues seem to be more understanding than those in Meaux.

"My father…" I say between two sobs, "It is my father, he rapes me…"

Rape. It is the first time I dare say the word. The first time I have managed to denounce the crime. And the word has the effect of a bomb. In the living room, a heavy silence settles in.

"Do you have papers?" one of the policemen finally asks.

"No. My passport is still over there."

"So we will have to go and get it…"

"No! I don't want to see them again!"

The policemen seem to hesitate for a moment.

"Do you know where your passport is?"

"In my bag, in my room, in the cellar…"

A short consultation follows. Two policemen decide to go to the Chemin des Petits-Chênes to pick up my passport while the third stays here with me. The two policemen go out and the car shoots off at top speed. When they come back a few moments later, they announce right away that they are empty-handed.

"Your father refuses to let us enter," the policeman explains. "He says that you are lying, that you have never been abused… He maintains that he doesn't understand what we are telling him."

"The only solution, Tina," the other policeman says, "is for you to come with us to your house. We can go into the house with you to get your passport. Don't worry, no one will touch you."

I am very scared, but these men seem to know what they are doing. I tell myself that they must certainly have experience and I get into the car with them. When we stop in front of the house, Godwin opens the door.

"What is happening again?" he asks.

"We are accompanying your daughter who wishes to get her identity papers," one of the officers explains.

"What is this all about?"

"She accuses you of abuse and rape," says one of the policeman curtly.

Without a word, without a glance at my adoptive father, I head towards the house and move directly down the cellar. The policeman escorts me. I take my passport and we go back up. Halfway up, I hear shouting.

"That's my daughter. You have no right! She is a minor!"

Trembling with fear, I don't dare take another step.

"Go on," the policeman behind me says. "You have nothing to fear. We will protect you whatever happens."

When we arrive in front of him, Godwin is crazy with anger. The calmness of the policeman in front of him seems all the more impressive.

"If you think that we are in the wrong, Monsieur Okpara, we invite you to follow us to the police station. We will take your statement…"

I can't believe it! Someone dares stand up to Godwin. Not only does this policeman glare at him, but he also does not step back when Godwin moves towards him in a threatening manner. Finally, Godwin moves aside to let us pass.

At the police station, the policemen settle me in an office upstairs. One of the three men who came to get me at the doctor's house sits down beside me. He has a tired, handsome face.

"We are looking for a shelter to host you," he tells me.

I don't dare reply that I haven't the least idea what a shelter is. I imagine that it is a place where people with problems like me can go. If it is difficult to find a place, that means that there must be a lot of other Tinas… I thought I was the only one in the world to suffer to this extent.

"Today, you see, is my last day of work," the policeman continues. "I should have left already. When we came to get you, it was my last intervention before the holidays." He looks at me and smiles.

"Don't worry," he adds. "I won't leave as long as I know you are not yet in safety."

I open my eyes wide. I want to engrave his face forever in my memory. It has been so long since I have seen a good man!

———————

Sitting in the office, curled up on a chair, my head between my hands, I attempt in vain to calm down my mind. Impossible to line up two ideas. It has been four years that I have been a slave in the Chemin des Petits-Chênes villa. Four years, four times three hundred and sixty-five days and each one of these days was made only of work, insults, blows and suffering. And here everything stops, here, now, in the space of just a few minutes. It is too extraordinary for me to believe it. I have been betrayed and disappointed so often that I still expect a last sudden twist in the film of my life.

I am alone in the office with a policeman in plain clothes. I get the feeling that he is a chief, a high-level officer, because of his age, his great presence and the way in which the others speak to him. I'm not crying any more. I wait. If fate thumbs its nose at me one more time, I think that it will be the last. Afterwards, there can only be death.

"Do you know these people?"

The voice of the policeman makes me raise my head. He is standing across from the office window overlooking the ground floor.

"Come and look, there is no risk to you."

I walk up timidly. I glance down and jump back just as quickly. Linda! Mamie! The two of them are there, downstairs! They came to get me! I was right to think that I could not be saved. My life is a rigged game. I cannot win.

I guess what is going to happen: the policeman will take me downstairs and I will be eligible for the same show as in Meaux. "Oh, Tina! We have been so scared for you! We are so happy to have found you!" And the policemen will let me leave with them. Back at the house, the tigresses will kill me.

Well, too bad. Or rather, so much the better! I will go and join my Mama. I will go to paradise. We have the right to paradise when we have been so miserable.

"This is your adoptive family?" the policeman asks.

"Yes."

"Do you want to see them?"

"Never again!"

"Are you sure?"

"Sure! Yes! Yes! Yes! Never again!"

He looks at me and I try to see in his face what he is thinking. Without a word he heads for the door and leaves the room. I glance again, ready to jump back if Linda or Mamie turn and raise their head in my direction. The policeman goes up to them and talks to them. I cannot hear what he says. Linda gesticulates. Is she protesting? Is she demanding that I be returned to them? I will never know.

Because a few moments later, she leaves the police station, with Mamie trotting on her heels. And I stay behind.

Fate! Cursed fate! It's over! This time, I am the one who wins!

———————

It is night when we leave the police station in a car. We drive a long time or at least, I get that impression and that reassures me. The further away I am from the Okpara family, the safer I will be. The car finally stops in front of a large house. A few moments ago, I saw a signpost indicating Bois-d'Arcy.

We were expected, because a woman comes out to meet us. After having spoken to the policemen in exchange for some papers, she leads me inside to a large room in the house. Tables are lined up and, in the back, there is a television on. Women are gathered around the screen.

"I guess you haven't eaten?" the woman asks me. "Are you hungry?"

Indeed, my stomach is rumbling. The woman sits me down at a table and a plate and cutlery are set in front of me. I will never forget this first meal! In the plate are steaming hot pasta and a beautiful lump of steak. I sit for several minutes without daring to touch the dish. This piece of smoking steak that smells so delicious seems too perfect, too good for me. Perhaps one cannot understand, when one hasn't lived through what I have lived through.

Never, in all of these years, did I have the right to such a piece of meat.

I cut a piece and bring it to my mouth. This steak has a marvellous taste, the taste of freedom!

13

Rose-tinted glasses…and black shadows

After the meal, a social worker takes me to a room that is already occupied by two other girls.

"This is Tina," she says. "She is going to spend some time with us…"

I enter, a little intimidated. There are three beds in the room. Two bunk beds and one single bed. It makes me feel so odd to live with girls of my own age, it has never happened to me before. The day had been so nerve-racking that I fall asleep as soon as I lie down. The next morning, when I open my eyes, it takes me a few minutes to realize that I am not in the cellar in Chatou. I see daylight through the shutters. What time could it be? How long have I slept? I remain lying down on the bed, not daring to get up.

"Are you okay?" one of my roommates asks me.

I make a sign to say yes. She doesn't ask anything more. In the days that follow, I will notice that here, each one has her load of misfortune. Each one knows how to respect the pain of the other. We listen to those who want to speak. We console those who cry. But we don't ask questions. Ever.

Soap and clean clothes are brought to me. After break-fast—again a new idea for me—a staff member leads me to the director's office. The director explains how my life is going to be here in this shelter at Bois-d'Arcy. Between the legal and medical appointments, I will have no time to be bored…

———————

Three days after my arrival, I return to the police station where a young girl takes my statement. She apologizes in advance, because she has some hard questions to ask me. The law requires precision. The word "rape" is not suffi-cient. There have to be precise details, to know how, how often, to what extent… penetration, fellatio, ejaculation. The words shock me: synonyms of pleasure for my torturer and of pain for me. They simultaneously express his satis-faction and my disgrace. Even so, I reply. Crying, again. Searching for words still. Mixing English and French. I am a pitiful victim who cannot even articulate her suffering. I will never manage. All the same, the policewoman notes my answers with a great deal of patience.

To verify my declarations, I am taken a bit later to see a gynaecologist. Another time, I am taken to the hospital at Versailles where I get x-rays and dental exams. This time, it is my age that they want to verify. Do they not believe me when I say I am seventeen years old? Finally, I go to see a psychiatrist regularly. A tall woman with red hair. Her soft voice and her way of explaining the most complicated things with simple words lead me to trust her. In her office, located in the shelter itself, there are two comfortable armchairs facing each other. Between the armchairs, there is a coffee table and on this table, there is always a box of tissues. Because there is a lot of crying in the psychiatrist's office.

She brings up a subject, asks me one or two questions, and then lets me talk. I release my memories to her, burning like acid, as they come to me all jumbled up, it doesn't matter. It doesn't take long for me to ask if I can take a tissue from the box.

These sessions leave me empty, exhausted, without strength, but relieved. I feel lighter. This woman listens to me, without judging me, without criticizing me. She even explains to me why I have such feelings. She reassures me too. For the first time in a long time, I am a human being like any other.

When I have nothing to do, I like to go into the garden to read among the fruit trees. Often, the letters blur before my eyes. If an educator surprises me in my sorrow, she comes quickly to comfort me.

"Why are you crying Tina? They are no longer here. They will never again hurt you. No one will hurt you now."

I wipe my tears repeating to myself: "I am free, I am free!"

One morning, Martine, the head social worker, comes to find me in my room. She seems disturbed.

"I have something to tell you," she begins. "Your parents have been arrested... It was on TV last night."

The newspapers also announce the arrest of Godwin and Linda Okpara. I discover the articles bearing a photo of my adoptive father in the Paris Saint-Germain outfit. The reporters make it clear that he has been indicted for rape and sexual violence by a person in a role of authority and for intentional violence against a minor. Linda was arrested for intentional violence against a minor and acts of torture and barbarism. Both have been incarcerated.

Linda and Godwin Okpara in prison! That seems unreal to me. Impossible. I am not the least bit relieved. On the contrary. I don't want Godwin to have troubles. He is rich, he is famous and people love him because he is a football player. Well, that's the way it is. So much the better for him. As for me, all I want now is to be able to start a new life. I just want to be happy. Above all, I fear for my family in Lagos, that through an error on my part, my father and my brothers may be victims of revenge.

Three weeks go by. I am just starting to get into my routine at the shelter in Bois-d'Arcy when Martine announces to me that I will have to leave. They find me sufficiently strong that I can take off on my own. I am able to leave the nest. I am going to live in a flat in Fontenay with three other girls...

Leaving the safety and softness of the shelter worries me a bit, but Martine gives me other big news. As of the beginning of September, I am going to vocational learning classes! I have decided to work hard to catch up on the lost years.

The flat in Fontenay is located in a "normal" building—what I mean is that the other residents are not people with problems like my three companions and myself. The flat has a kitchen, a big living room, and a corridor with two rooms on the right. We sleep two in a room. One last room, at the end of the corridor on the left, is an office for the staff—a man and a woman, that is to say a father and a mother, who look after us. They can, if they wish, sleep there on a folding bed.

Two or three days after my arrival, I finally discover the training centre. Julie, Ludovic and Daniel take care of us there. In the morning, we are taught French, maths and history. It looks like school and the joy that I have to be sitting there, in front of a notebook and a textbook, is indescribable. Once a week, we play sport. I believe that I am the happiest student in the world!

The afternoon is dedicated to a workshop. It is a large room where three or four people are already working. A radio plays music. The first day, Daniel greets me with a warm smile. He shows me the place to set myself up and explains to me that here we make jewellery that is then sold at fairs, exhibitions and other diverse events. He shows me different models and asks me which one I like. I point to a necklace with black, shining beads.

Daniel gives me the material and I set to work. It is a real pleasure. Not like the chores that I had to do at the Okpara's house. I am a bit clumsy at first, but thanks to Julie's advice, as she looks on from time to time, I progress rapidly. I manage to copy the model and am very proud of myself when the black beaded necklace is done.

"So… do you like it?" Julie asks me.

I have a hard time expressing the pride that I feel. The joy of making something beautiful with my hands is so strong…

"So, keep it," Julie continues. "It is a tradition in the workshop. We always keep the first jewellery that we make. It is a souvenir."

The girl with whom I share my room leaves the flat a short time after my arrival. Another replaces her straight away. Abused girls are not in short supply in this world. The new girl is African like me. She has the name of a queen of Egypt, Nefertiti, but she is from the Central African Republic. We quickly get along like two sisters. We like the same music, the same songs, and the same fashion… and sometimes we look at the same boys.

———

On 16 October 2005, for the first time in years, I celebrate my birthday. A youth worker gives me a package. Nefertiti laughs as she watches me rip open the wrapping paper. I discover a mini stereo inside. Something to listen to music with. For me alone. It belongs to me. I can't get over it.

The courses, the work at the workshop, life in the flat and Nefertiti's friendship, that is my life through rose-tinted glasses. But my life in black shadows has not disappeared. Pasted deep inside of me, bad memories seek out the least opportunity to resurface. Night is their opportune moment. Often, I wake up covered in sweat, my face drenched with tears. I catch my breath as if I have just run a sprint. Sitting on my bed, I remain with my eyes open in the dark, listening to the regular breathing of Nefertiti who is sleeping soundly.

I go back to bed, praying with all my might for the nightmare to leave me alone. It will come back, of course, today, tomorrow, another day or another night. Nothing and no one can erase these four years of suffering from my memory. All of this rubbish that has been dumped on me, in me, since I was twelve years old.

———————

I continue to see a psychiatrist. As much as the sessions with the house doctor at Bois-d'Arcy were good for me, these new sessions seem useless. The last psychiatrist that I saw, a man with white hair and a tired face, actually fell asleep while I was listing my sufferings. He woke up with a start and concluded the session saying:

"Well, what do you expect? That's life!"

I burst out laughing. What else could I do? Without a doubt he has become blasé with all the horrible stories he hears in his office. For me, I am not sure that it serves much of a purpose to go and see him. On the other hand, I am certain that it would do me so much good to have news of my family. When I talk to a trainer about that, she looks at me, astonished.

"But Tina," she says as naturally as possible, "the telephone is right there! Call your father!"

14

Misfortune strikes again

I must look like an idiot, frozen like a statue, with the telephone in my hand. In truth, I dare not dial my father's number. Finally, I take a deep breath and I start pushing the numbers. With the earpiece stuck to my ear, I listen to the ring that echoes far, far away. Once. Twice. Click! Over there, thousands of kilometres from Fontenay, someone picks up the telephone.

"Hello?"

It is the voice of Simon Omaku!

"Papa?"

"Tina!"

All at once, I realize that I have a billion things to tell him. Where should I start? I don't even remember any more what I wanted to tell him… and on his side, he stammers with joy and repeats my name, again and again. We laugh and cry at the same time. It lasts like that for two or three minutes before we finally start a real conversation.

Then, what he tells me shocks me completely. On several occasions, he ran into Linda Okpara when she went to Nigeria. When he asked for news about me, she replied that I went to school, that I was doing well and so on and so forth. She told him that I had projects for the future and that I'd have no problem getting into a major university.

"They are going to pay for what they did to you," he tells me.

It warms my heart to hear his voice and it is a relief to know that he has confidence in me. He knows that I did not misbehave. How I would love to see him and give him a kiss!

————————

In mid-October, an educator brings me a sheet of paper on which there is a list of names. He explains that I have to choose a lawyer to defend me in the trial. I glance at the list. All of the names are unknown to me. I place my finger randomly on the second line. Chance has just designated the solicitor Martine Peron as the one who will have the difficult task of defending me and confronting Godwin and Linda Okpara at the trial.

A few days later, an educator takes me to her office in Versailles by car, just a few steps away from the famous castle of Louis XIV, the Sun King.

My French has improved, but I still dread not understanding everything that is said at these appointments with the law. People often forget that I am an Anglophone and they speak quickly or use complicated words whose meanings I don't grasp. I have to make a major effort to concentrate in order not to get lost.

That day, fate decides to lend me a hand. Madame Peron's assistant is married to a British man and speaks English perfectly. She is a lifesaver for me. While I sit in the waiting room, the two of us talk. Speaking in English with her allows me to relax a bit.

Finally, Madame Peron arrives. I slip a shy hand in hers and I follow her into her office. Under her blond fringe, she has a look full of candour. Sitting across from her, I listen to her speak. Her voice is gentle, level-headed. She takes the time to explain the chronology of events and the steps that I will have to take before reaching the trial. At each important point, she makes sure that I have understood. I am impressed by her intelligence and all the work that she is doing for me. When we leave, I am relieved, persuaded that my future is in good hands. For the first time, I no longer feel alone in the face of the law.

———————

I ask the trainers again for the permission to use the phone. This time, I call Belgium, a bit worried, truthfully. I ask myself how I will be greeted when I announce myself.

"Magda? It's Tina…"

I am afraid that she will hang up. Afraid that she will blame me for having sent my adoptive parents to prison. Afraid that she will reject me and take the side of her friend, Godwin. Afraid that she will detest me. That is why I hesitated and waited so long before calling her. I even almost abandoned the idea, but I had to know. I had to tell her. I had to tell my dear Magda in my own words that I couldn't take it any more.

"Tina! I am so happy to hear your voice!"

The two of us talk. Then we are quiet at the same time and there is a deep silence on the telephone. What happiness to find Magda again!

"I am with you Tina," she tells me. "My house is wide open to you. You can come here whenever you want!"

My heart leaps. Magda! My dear Magda! If she could only know how these words warm my heart. She is not rejecting me. On the contrary, she is opening her arms wide. We talk a bit. She wants to hear my news, how I'm doing, what I do with my days... I tell her about the shelter, the classes and the workshop. Is everyone nice to me? Oh, yes! The trainers only scold me when they see me reading a Danielle Steel book in English. They'd like me to read in French!

"It is Christmas soon," she says. "Why don't you come and spend the holidays with us?"

Christmas at Magda's! What a dream.

And the dream becomes reality very quickly. It is cold enough to crack rocks when I take the train at the Gare du Nord. Propped up against the window, I watch the frozen landscape go by. I doze a bit. Finally, the train stops at the Brussels train station. On the platform I move forward with the other travellers, looking for Magda. There she is!

She has come to get me with her daughter. They wave at me...

My trip to visit them is indeed like a dream, a big dream full of warmth and love. We go and watch a football game in which her son Peter is playing. Then I accompany their daughter Sophie to a tennis match. And later, like two old girlfriends we go shopping together in town. The shop windows are lit up and the streets are decorated, it is an enchanting scene. Magda accompanies me to the shops. I look, amazed, at the beauty products, the clothes. Magda insists on giving me pyjamas in the colours of the Anderlecht football team.

That's how it was during my stay: a competition to see who could make me the happiest. Patrick takes me to an amusement park. I spend the whole day on the carousels and the roller-coaster. All of a sudden, everything is magic, everything is beautiful, everything is fun. As for Magda, she wants us to go and eat at the seaside. At the restaurant, I get dizzy discovering the prices on the menu. But Magda smiles and tells me not to worry: it is their treat. Back at their house, her son gets the idea of giving me a musical education! He makes me listen to a stack of CDs, young groups that I'm not familiar with. And when I like a song, he gives it to me!

When I get back to my flat in Fontenay, I have a treasure stored inside: my first Christmas and happy memories.

At the beginning of March, my Uncle Bala calls me.

"Your father is sick," he tells me. "He is in the hospital."

The hospital! Right away I think of my mother. She also went to the hospital and she died there!

"What is happening? Is it serious?" I ask my uncle.

"We don't know," he answers. "He has a lot of pain in his stomach…"

As much as I question my uncle, he cannot tell me any more. We have to wait until the doctors find out what my father has. Over the coming days, I jump every time the phone rings. I am waiting for news of my father, crazy with worry.

The call I so dread ends up coming through. It is again my Uncle Bala who calls.

"Tina," he begins, "you are a big girl now."

The tone of his voice worries me.

"I have something serious to tell you," he continues. "You know, we come into life, we go on our path, and then we leave. That is our destiny… all of us."

I understand! Oh, yes, I understand, but I refuse to believe it. It is not possible. It would be too unfair!

"You have to be strong, Tina," my uncle says again.

The words spoken next echo in my head. My father is dead! Deceased! Buried! Everything is over.

"What happened?" I stammer.

My uncle explained that my father had a very swollen stomach. The doctors attempted an operation. In vain. The surgeons were not able to relieve his problems or to understand what he was suffering from.

"They even wondered if Simon was poisoned," my uncle said.

I ask myself immediately if Godwin's admirers would not have gone after him because of me. "After the operation, your father was still in as much pain," my Uncle Bala continues. "The doctors called Emmanuel to explain the situation to him. Either they operated on your father again or they let him go. Your brother had to make a decision. He went to Simon's bedside and repeated what the doctors had told him. Your father told Emmanuel, 'Let me leave.' He died on 25 March, Tina. Before leaving, his last thoughts were for you. He only thought about all the hurt that was done to you… all this pain. He said 'I did not see my daughter again…'"

A long time after my uncle has hung up, I stay there, shattered, crying, the telephone in my hand. Francis, an educator, takes the receiver from my hand and hangs up for me.

"My father is dead," I tell him.

"If you like, you can go to Lagos for the funeral."

I shake my head.

"Everything is over," I say. "My father is dead and buried. Everything is over. It is useless now…"

———————

Madame Peron informs me at the beginning of June 2006 that I am summoned for a series of confrontations. She explains to me how things are going to proceed. I am going to find myself in an office, in the presence of a judge. Policemen will go and get the people accused of doing me wrong from prison, one by one. The judge will ask questions to confirm our respective statements. Peron reassures me or rather attempts to reassure me. I have nothing to fear. No one will be able to hurt me. All that I have to do is answer questions, to confirm what I already told the policemen who led the investigation.

"I will be right next to you," she tells me again. "To begin smoothly, I asked the judge to start with the confrontation with Madame Campbell."

With Mamie, it will be a bit like training. I feel relieved with the thought that Madame Peron masters the legal proceedings such that she can choose the order of the confrontations. I feel like I am the mistress of my destiny.

On 15 June 2006, Madame Peron and I enter the judge's office. A woman invites us to take our places in the seats in front of her desk. I sit down right in front of the magistrate, with Madame Peron on my left. On my right, there are two empty chairs. I know that, in a moment, Mamie and her lawyer will be seated there. The clerk of the court is sitting in front of a typewriter, a bit further away on my right.

The door of the office, behind my back, stands open. I hear footsteps and I turn around. What I see makes my blood run cold.

15

Confrontations

In the open doorframe, there where I was expecting to see Mamie arrive, Linda Okpara appears! Accompanied by two policemen, she steps firmly in my direction, her face closed, full of vengeance and disdain. Decidedly, nothing or no one can make the head of this woman bow.

I am panic-stricken. It wasn't planned like this! Madame Peron seems as surprised as I am and asks the judge:

"Was it not Madame Campbell who was summoned today?"

"We cannot always have what we wish," the magistrate replies.

My lawyer turns to me.

"At least, afterwards, the worst will be behind us," she whispers.

Linda enters the office and holds out her bound wrists to the police officers. They take off her handcuffs and she sits down on my right, just a few metres from me. The judge looks at her watch. She seems in a hurry.

"It is 2.55 pm," she says. "Is Madame Cotta not here? Too bad, we will begin without her."

Since Linda came into the room, it is as if I am paralyzed. Luckily. Otherwise, I would have been capable of throwing myself out the window to get away from her. With my eyes glued to the end of my shoes, I try to catch my breath. A weight crushes my chest, preventing me from breathing. I sense evil waves and Linda's hatred pressing down on me. I must not turn my head in her direction. I must not meet her eyes with mine. Otherwise, she will break my will and do with me as she pleases.

Madame Peron, on her side, does not seem the least bit destabilized. She faces up to Linda with a serenity that impresses me.

The judge asks the court clerk to read the statements that I made to the police. When she begins to read, I see myself again at the police station, in front of the young policewoman who was questioning me. I remember her first name, Virginie. She apologized for having to ask me such hard questions. That time too I ended up in tears.

The reading of my statement is interrupted by the arrival of Linda's lawyer. In the space of a second, I finally dare to look in the direction of my adoptive mother. Her eyes shoot out lightning bolts. As the clerk of the court has finished reading, the judge asks me if I confirm my statement.

"Yes… everything happened like that," I say.

Then it is time for Linda's declarations that the clerk of the court reads aloud. I discover that, to the police, Linda denies everything of which she is accused. She never treated me badly, never hit me, and never tortured me! If I was not in school, it was because I took classes at home over the Internet.

All of these lies she confirms today with an unbelievable nerve.

Madame Peron then passes on the offensive. Each of her questions is like a missile that she fires at Linda Okpara. I am still trembling. I get the feeling that my adoptive mother is going to jump up and break everything in the office.

"You were often travelling, Madame Okpara," Madame Peron says. "Who did the housework at your home in your absence?"

"My aunt, Madame Campbell, she was there for that!" Linda replied.

"Did Tina have to help her?"

"I don't know! I wasn't there. If someone made Tina work, it was not me who ordered it. I was not aware of everything that happened in my absence."

It is a real trial of strength that takes place between the two women. They confront each other with their eyes, with their voices. Madame Peron doesn't give an inch.

"Who did the laundry? Who did the shopping? Who ironed?" she asks.

"Mamie! Mamie! Mamie!" Linda repeats.

I should lift my head up, sit up straight in my chair and make this liar shut up! But there is a weight crushing me and I am incapable of the slightest movement, the tiniest word. I tell myself that Linda won the match a long time ago. She broke me.

"Did you hit Tina?" Madame Peron asks.

"No," Linda answers. "I never raised a hand against her."

"Not even when she wasn't well behaved? Or when she didn't obey you?"

"Tina was always a difficult child," Linda answers.

And I feel her eyes on me, even more insistent.

"Her father came to see me in Lagos to complain. He couldn't do anything with her. She only caused him problems. A real bitch that fought with everyone in his house!"

I hear the typewriter clicking while the clerk of the court captures all of these lies. This cuts into my heart. My father couldn't have said that about me.

"He asked me to take her with me! He begged me!" Linda continues. "He said that I was the only one who could do something with her. That I had to take charge of her. She wasn't ten years old and you know what her father told me? That she was a pervert! She slept with everyone!"

A heavy silence follows Linda's declarations. I would like to be able to read the thoughts of the adults around me, the lawyers and the magistrate. They are intelligent. They went to university. Are they really going to believe all of these horrors? It is my word against that of Linda Okpara. Who are they going to believe? The child or the adult? The little orphan from Nigeria or the wife of the football player from PSG?

I am in shock. Madame Peron must notice because she tries to calm me down. She tells me that I must not be scared, that people are here now to protect me. I have already heard these arguments so many times, but it doesn't stop the fear from eating away at my brain like a cancer.

I have the weekend to recover from this ordeal, but by Monday afternoon, I am back in front of the judge's desk. This time, I am confronted with my adoptive father.

He also objects outright to everything that he is accused of and calls me a liar. He doesn't shout like his wife. He doesn't spit out insults or curses. His method of defence is nevertheless the same as Linda's. He dirties me, his victim.

On the housework, he remains vague, implying that those are women's issues, therefore not in his domain. His only responsibility was football. Madame Peron asks him the same questions as Linda.

"Who did the washing, ironing and vacuuming?"

Answer: he doesn't know. Madame Peron asks again. "Who took care of the children?"

"Mamie, most of the time," he replies.

"You don't think that that is a lot of work for a sixty-five-year-old woman, Monsieur Okpara?" Madame Peron asks.

"I don't know…"

"With the comfortable salary that you earn, you never thought of hiring a housekeeper?"

He shrugs. The judge next asks him his version of the rapes of which I accuse him. Godwin looks sidelong at me and affirms that he never touched me.

"Your wife surprised you while you were having sexual relations with your daughter," the magistrate reminds him.

"It was Tina who trapped me," he replies without batting an eyelid. "That day, I was tired after training and I had been drinking. Vodka. I was drunk and I went to lie down to rest. Tina came to join me… she started doing things to me and before I could push her away, my wife arrived."

Each one of these lies is like a steamroller that goes over me. They are flattening me one after another. They push me under the ground.

After Linda, it is Godwin who condemns me. Two adults against a girl. Two rich and powerful people against the living dead. It is a fight that I can only come out of defeated. Madame Peron may well have tried to make me feel better leaving the judge's office, but I see everything in black. I feel heavy black clouds gathering above my head, sensing that the storm that will end up exploding above me will be fatal. There remains one hope, a last maybe. Mamie. As of the next day, we will find ourselves face to face. Far from the influence of Linda, far from her threats, she will perhaps dare to finally tell the truth and come to my rescue.

It is a strange confrontation that begins Tuesday, 20 June 2006 at precisely 2.45 pm in the judge's office. I am sitting in front of the magistrate with Madame Peron on my left, the same place I was in for the previous sessions. Mamie arrives with her defence lawyer and a translator because she claims that she understands neither French nor English. Everything that is said in the office therefore has to be repeated to her in Yoruba. The session is broken up, disjointed, tiresome… Mamie complains a lot and presents herself as a victim. As for the abuse and torture I was subjected to, she doesn't know anything. It is clear that she has no intention of telling the truth.

At the end of this last confrontation, I exhale a sigh of relief. At least one challenge is over…

I know the next step. The trial at the criminal court. I will again have to face my torturers then. This time they will all three be together in the witness box and they will repeat their lies. I turn to Madame Peron. One question burns on my lips.

"Will the trial be as hard as the confrontations?"

16

The last trial

Tuesday, 29 May 2007. I discover the setting where the last legal act of my story will take place: the Court of Versailles. In this large room with its mahogany panelling and white marble tiled floors, my adoptive parents will be judged. The trial should last four days.

I sit in the first row, next to my lawyer. Seated across from me is the judge, Madame Foncelle, a woman of about fifty, dressed in the long red magistrate's robe, but to my great surprise, she has short hair. Remembering an old film, I was expecting to discover a judge in a ridiculous wig, banging a wooden mallet for silence like in the Court of Louis XIV.

I turn towards the room while the benches for the public fill up. I am looking for Nefertiti in the crowd. My room-mate insisted on coming along to support me. Two teachers, Sylvia and Francis, are here too. Their presence reassures me a bit. This morning, I didn't even know how to dress to go to court. Sylvia suggested being natural, so I wore a pair of jeans, a white shirt and a black jacket.

I am surprised to see so many people. The court is swarming with reporters attracted by Godwin's notoriety.

A former football player from PSG on trial is not common. A group from television arrives with the camera on their shoulder to film me. I refuse and they move away, annoyed. Later these journalists will be outside looking for me at the exit of the court, lying in wait between two cars to film me on the sly. I have too many other concerns to worry about them right now.

For the moment, the dock is still empty. In the front, a bunch of lawyers in black gowns settle in. The first, a poorly shaved man with a round face will defend Mamie. Madame Peron explains to me that the two others, a bald man and a brown-haired woman with glasses on top of her head, are well-known lawyers.

"Better than you?" I ask her.

"More well known than me in any case," she tells me with a smile.

Suddenly, a noise runs through the crowd. The door of the dock has just opened. A policeman appears with Godwin on his heels. He is wearing a white polo shirt. Linda is just behind him, looking very elegant in a leather jacket and braided hair. She turns her head and scans her eyes up and down the room as if she is looking for someone. Her eyes stop when they meet mine and a wicked smile forms on her lips. I try to calm myself down, because I am trembling all over. I think again about the advice that Sylvia gave me just before coming into the court. "If they scare you, remember that you do not have to look at them!" I pretend to observe the presiding judge, across from me, following her every move with my eyes. Next to her, I notice a member of the jury looking at me with a nasty look. He looks furious…

Then Mamie arrives. Unlike my adoptive parents, she is not incarcerated and appears before the judge as a free woman. She seems lost when entering the courtroom and a policeman has to show her the bench where she should sit just in front of the dock.

The judge then adjusts her glasses on her nose and announces that we are going to have the reading of the evidence pertaining to the case. Madame Peron explains to me that this is the document that summarizes all of the facts about the events and actions for which the defendants are accused including the investigation itself and even the psychiatric evaluations of the defendants. Head lowered, I listen to this terrible story that is mine. I don't dare to lift my eyes. I feel everyone looking at me…

When the court clerk completes the reading and the judge calls the first witnesses, I am stunned like a boxer after a fight. I follow the beginning of this hearing as if in a fog. People arrive, place themselves a few metres from me in front of the witness stand, a glass plaque topped by a chrome bar, then the judge asks them questions, they reply, and then leave, without even giving me the time to identify them or to remember the role they played in my existence. Nevertheless, one face suddenly appears familiar to me. Who is this man? I search in my memory. The word "kindness" comes to me. Oh, yes! I remember! The man who is testifying in front of the jury is the policeman who postponed his departure on holiday to attend to me. He explains in what circumstances he picked me up with his colleagues and then sends me one last benevolent look and goes to sit with the public. I realize that I do not even know the name of this man who was so good to me. Other policemen come next to explain how they arrested Godwin.

"We presented ourselves at his house in Chatou," an inspector explains. "Monsieur Okpara opened the door himself. When we explained to him that we were coming to take him in for questioning, he turned towards his children and said to them 'Say nothing! Answer nobody!'"

I have no difficulty recognizing the next witness. It is Sonia who goes up to the witness stand, Mamie's friend's daughter.

"In what circumstances did you meet the Okpara family?" the judge asks her.

"We met at the Mormon church," Sonia replies. "My mother had got along well with Madame Campbell, the grandmother…"

"Did you know in what conditions their daughter Tina lived?"

"I know that she slept in the cellar, because I followed her there one day."

"How was she dressed?" the judge continues.

"Out of fashion!"

"Old-fashioned? What do you mean?"

Sonia doesn't answer. The presiding judge examines her jogging pants and white tank top.

"And you," she encourages, "How would you define your outfit today?"

"Me? I'm in fashion!"

Her naïve response sets off a few laughs. Even I surprise myself by smiling.

It doesn't matter. Everyone understood what she meant and that's the important point. Plus, she lets me relax slightly.

The judge consults a paper in the file open in front of her. Then she calls the next witness. When I hear her name, my heart leaps into my throat!

The door opens and suddenly it is as if everything is disappearing around me, the court, the crowd, the judges, the lawyers, and even the defendants in the dock. The whole scene melts into a misty magma through which Magda walks out of. She advances slowly, as if she was afraid to come to the witness stand, between Godwin and me.

Upon the request of the judge, she states her identity and then the cross-examination begins. Magda reports, first of all, the circumstances that led her to keep the company of the Okpara family. Football. The ties created bit by bit that lasted after Godwin's transfer to a French club. Finally, the questions are about me.

"Did you know that Tina was battered by her adoptive parents?" the judge asks.

"I noticed that she was treated differently than the other children," Magda replies.

"What do you mean by 'differently'?" the judge asks.

"She worked all the time, from morning to night… which didn't prevent her adoptive mother from yelling at her."

"Two-faced bitch!"

In the dock, Linda stands up and points a furious finger at Magda.

"You came to my house! You were my guest! You took advantage of me!" she yells.

Her lawyer tries to calm her down.

"Madame Okpara! Sit down and leave the witness alone!" the judge orders.

"You said you were my friend!" Linda shouted. "And you come here to talk badly about me! Traitor! Liar!"

The police officers seize Linda. She sits down. The features of her face are deformed with rage. Next to her, Godwin is holding his head in his hands.

Now it is Linda's turn to be questioned.

"In what circumstances did you adopt Tina?" the judge asks her.

"She was the daughter of a friend in Lagos, in Nigeria," Linda answers. "Her mother had died. Her father didn't know what to do with her. She slept with everyone, even her brother. She was prostituting herself when she was not yet nine years old. He begged me to take her with me. He claimed that I was the only one who could manage her."

"Did you buy Tina?" the judge asked.

Buy me? I had never imagined for one moment that I could have been bought like a thing or an animal!

"No!" Linda replied.

The judge looks in her file and gets out a piece of paper. She turns to Godwin.

"You declared during the investigation to have given thirty thousand naira, the equivalent of three hundred and seventy-five euros, to Tina's father in two payments…"

"That was to help him," Godwin answers. "I gave him that money because I liked him and he wanted to buy a motorcycle."

On the stand, Linda and Godwin continue to answer the judge. I no longer care about any of this. The questions. The answers. The statements of this person and that person. All of this has no more meaning for me. The only thing that counts is this revelation that shatters me. I was bought! They sold me! Three hundred and seventy-five euros! How could my father have done such a thing? I barely notice that the hearing is over and everyone is heading towards the exit. Nefertiti, Sylvia and Francis join me and stand around me. I don't hear them. I don't see them any more. A storm has erupted in my head! Lightning! Thunder! I can only think about one thing: thirty thousand naira, three hundred and seventy-five euros! For those people, that was all that I was worth… That is the price of my life!

———————

The hearing resumes with the video recording of my statement in the office of the investigating magistrate. The lawyers for the defence are against it, but Madame Peron stands firm.

"That is part of the evidence!" she insists.

She did not raise her voice, but she carries the argument and Judge Foncelle asks that we start the viewing. I have changed so much physically that I have a hard time believing it is me on this screen. Hearing my voice hurts me and I fall apart again. I am in tears twice over. I am crying on the screen and I am crying in the hearing.

The screen finally goes dark and—here is the moment that I have been dreading so much—the judge calls Mademoiselle Tina Okpara to the witness stand.

I feel Linda's eyes on me, like during the confrontation.

"Can you describe your days in the house in Chatou?" the judge begins.

She speaks softly. I see that she is trying to handle me carefully. I answer, my throat tight, my voice broken with emotion.

"I got up at five o'clock in the morning. I prepared the affairs of the children. I woke them up and gave them their breakfast. Then I took them to school. I run back home, otherwise I risked making my mother angry. Afterwards, I vacuumed and then I mopped and prepared lunch. In the afternoon, I washed the clothes, by hand, because I wasn't allowed to use the washing machine…"

"Why not?" the judge asks, astonished.

"My mother said I was too stupid… Afterwards, I ironed and cooked. I also had to take care of the garden. I was never in bed before midnight."

"Were you hit?" the judge asks.

"The grandmother slapped me. Monsieur Okpara hit me too, but it was his wife who hit me the most often and with anything: garden tools, kitchen appliances, shoes…"

"That's not true! That's all a bunch of lies. She was treated like the others! She lived and ate like the others!"

Once again, Linda was standing in the box.

"Look at me!" she screams specifically at me. "Look at me, you liar, and dare repeat what you just said!"

I then turn in her direction. I know that she can no longer reach me. Tonight I will not go back to her house. I suddenly feel stronger.

"I am no longer scared of you," I tell her, holding her stare.

"You never went to school, right?" the judge continues.

"Never. That was the worst for me. I was brought from Nigeria after having been promised that I would go to school and instead of that..."

"Madame Okpara," the judge said turning to the dock, "Why did you never put your adopted daughter in school?"

"She was too stupid," Linda answers. "She didn't have the capacity, it would have served no purpose."

The judge turns back to me. She lowers her voice.

"Speak to us about what happened with Godwin Okpara," she says.

I have to again tell the story of my ordeal. I speak, broken and ashamed, about how Godwin took me down to the cellar. I explain the story at Christmas and the gas cylinder. I speak about all the other times...

The judge turns to Godwin: "Do you admit having had sexual relations with your adopted daughter?"

"It happened only once," Godwin replies. "At that time, I had left PSG and Standard didn't want to renew my contract. I had no club and I was worried about the future…"

"Your career does not interest us, Monsieur Okpara," the judge says, interrupting him. "I am asking you if you had sexual relations with Tina."

"That day, I had drunk three bottles of vodka," Godwin continues. "I am not accustomed to drinking alcohol, I felt bad… I wanted to go and lie down. Tina joined me in my room. I never forced her. In fact, I did not sleep with her, it was she who slept with me. It was the day that my wife surprised us."

"What happened when Madame Okpara arrived?" the judge asks me.

I am still crying, clutching the chrome bar.

"I ran away," I say, "but I didn't know where to go… so I came back to the house. Linda made me go up into the room and told me to take off all my clothes. She shaved my head… She went down into the kitchen and came back with a pipette full of spicy sauce…"

I continue my story. In the hearing, there are a few smothered wails. I am no longer the only one crying… I continue my testimony, whatever the cost, in tears, one word after the other.

"Linda went to get a razor blade, she cut me twice on the lower abdomen. When she left, she told me that I should not dirty her carpet with my blood."

There. I'm done. I have made it to the end of my story and return to my seat, near Madame Peron. In the room, the emotion is palpable. A long and heavy silence reigns, as if no one dares to speak. Finally, the judge addresses Linda sharply:

"Do you still deny having tortured Tina?"

"I am innocent! She is lying!"

The judge turns to Mamie.

"You were present that day, Madame Campbell... What do you have to say?"

"I don't know," Mamie begins in a whining tone of voice... "Linda told me that Tina had done some things with her father. I went to see Tina. She was crying a lot, so I took her in my arms."

"That's not true! You saw everything and you did nothing!"

This time, I am the one standing. I am astonished at myself. I was terrified before the trial and now, in the heat of the hearing, I am able to defend myself on my own.

"You always said you were a believer! A believer doesn't tell lies! So you must tell the truth today! You were there and you told me that we had to let her anger come out!"

"I know nothing," Mamie replied. "I swear on the Bible... I didn't see anything."

On Friday, 1 June 2007, the trial ends. I cried more tears in these four days than my body could hold. I have gone through so many strong emotions that I am completely worn out... Madame Peron, once more, has explained to me how events are going to proceed. The prosecuting counsel, Madame Chapelle, must speak first. She represents society and, in its name, she will demand the sentence that seems just to her.

"Tina was placed into slavery," she says, "worse even, this young girl was forced to satisfy the sexual urges of Godwin Okpara. He raped his own daughter for two years. And when she discovered this, Linda Okpara showed unbelievable brutality and sadism. I call for a sentence of ten to twelve years of criminal imprisonment for both of them. Against Madame Badejoko Campbell, who knew, who saw, who could have come to the rescue of Tina but who did nothing, I call for a sentence of three years, with thirty months suspended sentence."

Madame Peron rose in turn, very calm.

"In Nigeria, seventy-one percent of the population live on less than one dollar per day," she begins.

She speaks softly. Every word that she utters is carefully weighed.

"Tina lived with a modest family, but her parents met her basic needs and never did she complain about their poverty. There was always something to eat in her plate. But then her mother dies and tensions arise with her stepmother. It was then that Godwin and Linda Okpara come into the picture. They propose to adopt Tina. Perhaps there are pressures: after all, Tina's father has work and housing thanks to Godwin's godfather. In any case, promises are made: of a better future for Tina and a bit of money. Tina was not sold by her father, but she was bought by the Okpara couple who wanted to buy themselves a little maid."

In the room, you could have heard a fly buzz.

Even Linda, for once, remains silent.

"Who is Linda Okpara?" Madame Peron continues. "An intelligent woman, energetic, brilliant, but completely lacking in maternal love. She cannot love and only wants one thing: material success. She accumulates a fortune—four houses in Nigeria, the fifth under construction, a flat in New York, and the villa in Chatou—and pays no debts. She is also a domineering woman, who reigns as a despot over her husband, her children and her house. The slightest frustration or contradiction drives her to limitless anger."

Madame Peron turns towards the dock. Linda shoots her a black look.

"We have seen her 'not troubled' during this hearing, according to her lawyer."

Then Madam Peron attacks Godwin.

"He knew that Tina slept in the cellar. He treated her without consideration, letting her unload the wood and chop it, standing there with his arms folded… then he ends up raping her, more and more frequently, while hitting her, and threatening her... using her for all the practices that he doesn't do with his wife. Tina is at his mercy; he knows it and abuses her. Today, he denies the facts. He does not even have the courage to apologize for the wrong that he has done to this child."

And now it is Mamie's turn.

"She could have been a refuge for Tina. She preferred to be an instrument of Linda Okpara."

A pause. Madame Peron arrives at the end of her closing speech.

"They are all guilty," she says. "Guilty for having taken this child from her country, her family, her friends, her schooling... for having subjected her, in total dependence, in a foreign country for four and a half years, to inhumane conditions. In the terminology of French law, the word 'slavery' does not exist. So I will speak of a crime against humanity."

To conclude, she addresses the members of the jury, asking them to punish Godwin with twenty years of imprisonment and Mamie with ten. For Linda, she asks for life!

The bald lawyer, with his finely framed glasses, is next. Godwin's lawyer, Monsieur Joseph Cohen-Sabban, makes important-looking gestures to bolster his speech. When he spreads his arms he looks like a big black bird. He is truly formidable. He speaks of Godwin's childhood in poverty.

He calls him the "child with golden feet". The success, glory and money that have come upon him so rapidly thanks to football have made him lose his sense of moderation.

"His maturity and his thoughts did not develop," the lawyer says, pointing to Godwin in the dock. "This man was an exceptional player, but he had the mind of a twelve-year-old child. His wife dominated him, holding the reins of his life. And, in the end, he did not know how to consider Tina his daughter."

Madame Françoise Cotta also makes dramatic gestures with her arms. She walks back and forth, chanting the same refrain over and over: "It is not easy! It is not easy!" as if wanting to force this into the head of the members of the jury.

"It is not easy to be the descendant of a slave," she says. "It is not easy to be a poor girl, it is not easy to become rich all of a sudden, thanks to her footballer husband."

Listening to her, Linda has all the excuses and I am the guilty one!

Finally, Monsieur Florent Hauchecorne asks purely and simply for the acquittal of Mamie. According to him, there is nothing of consequence against her in the case.

I am suddenly seized by doubt. All of these speeches appear very impressive to me, even more so than that of my lawyer. These lawyers spoke longer and more loudly. What if Godwin and Linda get off in the end? What would happen to me? Would they send me back to their house? And what if everything started again, just as before?

The judge asks the defendants if they would like to add anything before the members of the jury leave to deliberate. Godwin gets up. He looks at me.

"I apologize for the hurt that I caused you and for the hurt that my family caused you," he says.

A pause. Then he adds a word, just one.

"Sorry," he says, before sitting back down.

"Madame Okpara?" the judge asks.

"I have nothing to say," she snarls.

The judge turns to me.

"Tina, would you like to say a few words?"

I get up, facing the defendants.

"It is not for me to judge them, it is the work of the law," I say. "I just want to be far away from them and never see them again. Ever. But I do not want them to go to prison because of me…."

———

The courtroom empties with a commotion. Linda and Godwin are led away by the police. I don't know what we have to do.

"We are going to go drink some coffee while waiting for the verdict," says Madame Peron.

We squeeze in together around a table in a brasserie not far from the court.

Nefertiti talks a lot. Sylvia is worried. How long does a jury deliberation last? Can Godwin and Linda be acquitted? And why this and why that? Madame Peron answers, advising that we be patient. I think again about the speeches.

Just before 8 pm, we are back in the courtroom. The members of the jury appear a few minutes later. Everyone is standing, waiting for the announcement of the verdict. There is an incredible tension, electricity in the air! I am anxious, horribly anxious. Then one of the members of the jury speaks at the request of the judge.

"Godwin Okpara: guilty! Linda Okpara: guilty! Badejoko Campbell: guilty!"

The judge announces the sentences herself. Fifteen years of imprisonment for Linda, thirteen years for Godwin, five years including four years suspended sentence for the grandmother.[5] I turn to Madame Peron, because I don't understand the French term for 'suspended sentence'. She is explaining this to me when suddenly screaming is heard. In the dock, Godwin is impassive. Linda, however, is dancing and screaming like a crazy woman. She bangs her forehead against the railing of the dock.

---

5   In February 2008, Godwin Okpara's sentence was reduced to ten years imprisonment by the court of appeal of the Hauts-de-Seine. Linda Okpara's sentence of fifteen years of imprisonment was confirmed. Mamie got a sentence of four years including eighteen months behind bars.

"Ladies and gentlemen!" she yells.

I don't understand what she says next, she utters threats whose meaning I don't grasp. The police officers attempt to control her.

"Thank you, Tina!" she still manages to shout.

"Thank you and good luck in France!"

The guards take her away. The shouts are quelled. It is over. This time, it is really over. The nightmare is over.

A man comes up to us. It is the member of the jury that looked at me strangely at the beginning of the trial. This time a broad smile brightens his face. He takes Madame Peron's hand in his and congratulates her warmly.

"Bravo, Maitre," he says. "Bravo…"

17

Survivor

I am strong and independent enough to live alone now. This is what the social workers and teachers tell me. They tell me that I can be proud of the path I have travelled. That is the case. I am proud, happy and sad at the same time. Happy because a new life is opening up before me, sad because I have to leave the welcoming and reassuring nest in Fontenay where I had my habits and my bearings.

I settle some time later in a studio flat. Twenty square metres in a calm neighbourhood. This time, no roommates nor friends. No social worker sleeping in the office on a folding bed. I have to learn to live alone. Or almost. Every night, a guard comes to knock on my door. If I don't answer, he uses a spare set of keys to enter and see if everything is okay. If he finds me sleeping, he closes the door again noiselessly and continues on his rounds. His presence is reassuring but prevents me from growing up. I have the fierce will to become a girl like any other. After a few days, I ask him not to stop by any more. Knowing that I can call him if there is a problem is enough for me.

———

I know that Godwin and Linda are behind bars. Alas, there is no prison in which to lock away my nightmares. At times, during the night, my horrible memories pierce my heart with their poisoned fangs.

In these moments, it is as if I am sent underground. I go down the steps of a staircase that is long, very long and I find myself in a grim and icy room that looks like the musty cellar of Chemin des Petits-Chênes. All around me hang paintings of my life. On one, our neighbour in Lagos is yelling out to me that my mother is going to die. On another, my father is kissing me goodbye at the airport. There are paintings of Godwin, one of him raping me, one where I have to ask him for forgiveness on my knees. The most numerous are those of Linda. Linda hitting me. Linda whom I must massage. Linda insulting me. Linda shaving my head. Linda torturing me with spicy sauce, Linda holding a razor blade…

This is my hell. I am the curator of this personal museum of horrors, condemned forever to look upon these monstrous paintings in my memory.

"Now what are you going to do?" People ask me this question often since the trial of my adoptive parents. I answer: "Become a nurse!" It appears impossible, inaccessible for a young girl who was not sent to school. But I am fighting and I work hard. In September 2006, I even take a test with one written component in French and I obtain a certificate issued by the Red Cross to become a caregiver for the elderly. Thanks to this, I am hired soon thereafter by a geriatric service. I discover what team spirit is like, the very particular ambiance of a medical service, the work with nurses and nursing aides…

At the centre, I make it a point of honour to always be cheerful and happy. Sadness is forbidden! I always work hard to bring joy and energy to the elderly people. A kind word, some extra attention, costs nothing and when, thanks to me, a smile brightens these lovely wrinkled faces, their hair suddenly looks less grey, their arms and legs less stiff and their voices less quavering, I am the happiest employee in the world. Their happiness is the best balm for healing the wounds of my soul. My only fear is seeing one of my dear patients disappear one day. Which, alas, occurs at times…

———

None of my colleagues knows my story. I want to be a girl like any other and I want neither pity, nor favourable treatment. I therefore hide my heavy past, which is not always easy.

One day, Aminata asks me if I want to go with her to do some shopping. I accept with joy. I like Aminata a lot. Working with her is pleasant and, little by little, we have discovered some similarities. I accompany her on this outing and soon there are others.

We have a lot of fun and we laugh. She asks me often, where do you come from, your origins? I answer by saying that I am from Nigeria. From Lagos. But there are lots of "holes" in my story and these holes intrigue Aminata. Her questions become more precise and her tone more insistent. I think about this a long time, the pros and cons, especially to judge if I can trust my new friend. One day, she asks me again and, this time, I decide to tell her everything. She listens without saying a word. Hearing the summary of my existence freezes her on the spot. She is petrified, stupefied. I think she thought I was hiding a painful secret, but not to this extent.

"I won't talk about this to anyone," she tells me. "I promise. Never. To anyone."

Aminata keeps her promise. Never has anyone learned about my terrible story from her mouth.

———————

The other difficulty is that Godwin Okpara's name is famous and PSG supporters have not forgotten him. Sometimes, when I say my name, the listener is astonished. "Okpara? Are you from the football player's family?" In those instances, I act like I don't know anything. What football player? Inevitably, my listener launches into explanations. "A player for PSG accused of raping his daughter and so on. He is in prison. You never heard of him?" "No. Never." I claim that Okpara is a very common name in

Nigeria. My story can thus come up anywhere, any time. A colleague invites me over one day with other girls from the centre for a raclette party that she is having at her place. I like this colleague a lot. She is a happy girl who is always joking around and teasing me gently about my bad French.

"For all this time you have been in France, Tina! You are really dumb!" she had the habit of saying.

She evidently couldn't know that she is sending me back to the black periods of my past. When Linda said to me that I wasn't clever enough to go to school, she also called me "dumb".

The evening of the raclette party, I find myself around a table with our colleagues, our hostess and a boy from her family. We talk about this and that. I can see the young man staring at me. Is it my family name? My face? He claims that he knows me without knowing where from or why. I am sure, on my part, that I have never met him before.

The evening ends. A few days later, at the centre, my colleague comes up to me.

"Come to the park," she says. "I have something to ask you…"

Knowing her, I am expecting a joke. But, on the contrary, her face is very serious. She retrieves a newspaper cutting from her pocket. The title jumps out at me: "Godwin Okpara condemned for the rape of his daughter."

"Is this you?" she asks.

What can I say? Deny it again?

"Yes, it is me," I say.

My colleague explains to me that her relative, convinced that he recognized me, set off to do some research and he ended up discovering this article. She is very sorry. She doesn't know what to say. She admits that her mind is on all the jokes that she has played on me. If she had only known… I reassure her. She couldn't have known and the jokes never hurt me. I want to be treated like anyone else. I do not want to remain the victim of Linda and Godwin Okpara forever!

I left the safe house where I had my studio flat. Where I live now there are no more guards, no more teachers nor social workers. The nightmares, on the other hand, are still there. The fear as well. It has even happened that I think I recognize Godwin Okpara in the street. I panicked thinking that he was out of prison and that he was coming to take revenge. It was a mistake of course… I was only the victim of a vague resemblance.

When I was still a prisoner in the cellar in Chatou, I remember having written one day, in my diary: "Will someone come along one day just to listen to me?" Since I have been free, I have met dozens of people who have listened to me. I even went home to Lagos and my brothers and my family welcomed me with open arms. All this love, all this warmth gives me an incredible energy and the strength to conquer my difficult challenge: to be a girl like any other.

Acknowledgements

I thank France, the country that freed me and gave me justice.

I thank Martine Peron, my lawyer, my guardian angel. She made me understand that it was not enough to speak loudly and to gesticulate to be heard.

I thank Madame Veronique Ayton, her assistant. Her smile and kindness are engraved forever in my memory.

I thank my brothers Emmanuel and Ayuba, my sister Esther, my Uncle Bala, my cousin Mica and all of my family in Nigeria… You have never forgotten me and your arms have remained open to me. You are and you will always remain my real family.

I thank Magda, Patrick and their children. They were my only light during those four years of darkness.

I thank Francis, Martine, Fizia, Dominique, Josette and all of the teachers and managers of the Service d'Acceuil d'Urgence de Bois d'Arcy and from the Centre d'Acceuil Educatif d'Insertion. At times, I forget your names but never your faces nor the dedication that you have shown towards me. You have given life back to me.

I thank Madame Garçonnet for her support at each moment.

I thank Monsieur and Madame Kalu, Mademoiselle Natacha Yoran Torde, Mademoiselle Nefertiti Pouenedela,

Mademoiselle Chantal Marboua… You are always available when I am having a hard time and when sorrow is weighing me down. I would lose my footing if I did not have you. This book is an opportunity to tell you just how much I love you. You mean so much to me.

Thank you also to Nathalie, who found me on the street, listened to me and guided my first steps towards freedom. I will never forget you.

From the bottom of my heart, thank you…